Jacob St.

D1336520

Bristol As It Was 1976 - 1980

What is there about that particular view
That merits the name of beauty? Is it
There in the scene, and apparent to you
As to me? Or do I read into the scene
Personal references, things much older
Than today and its pictures? Is beauty
Not only in the eye of the beholder,
But also in the mind, the hands, the heart,
Prejudging, focusing and making real
An image to be carried negatively
Until awareness and the sight and feel
Of something produce a positive picture?
And a past attitude will even dictate
Whether it shall be penny plain or coloured.

Photographic Memory, from
Loosing My Grip, selected poems
by Bill Pickard

(1) 23 March 1975: St Augustine's Parade Ivor Morris, coachman, and Wally Maddocks, footman, in full state livery driving the Lord Mayor to St Stephen's church on Palm Sunday. The pageantry of driving in state was deemed too expensive in 1991 and the Bristol state coach, built in 1850 by Bartons' of Quay Head [**9/27**], now rests in the Industrial Museum, save for very occasional use.

BRISTOL
As It Was
1976-80

Photographs from the
Reece Winstone Archive

by
John Winstone

Foreword by
David Dawson
formerly Curator of Archaeology at Bristol Museum

Reece Winstone Archive & Publishing
Ilex House, Front Street
Churchill, Bristol BS19 5LZ

For Rosie

The *Bristol As It Was* Series

by **Reece Winstone FRPS**

by **John Winstone RIBA**

*Those titles marked with an asterisk are out of print. The remainder
are available direct from the publishers, some in limited numbers.*

Abbreviations

B&GAS *Bristol & Gloucestershire Archaeological Society*
BDC *Bristol Development Corporation*
BIAS *Bristol Industrial Archaeology Society*
C16, C17 etc. *Sixteenth & seventeenth centuries etc.*
CAP *Conservation Advisory Panel*
CPAB *Council for the Preservation of Ancient Bristol*

EH *English Heritage, was* HBC *Historic Buildings Council*
MSC *Manpower Services Commission*
PBA *Port of Bristol Authority*
RCHM *Royal Commission on Historical Monuments*
RW *Reece Winstone*
SPAB *Society for the Protection of Ancient Buildings*

Cross references to other volumes are shown in bold type by
volume number followed by plate number viz [**2/135**]

ISBN 0 900814 74 8

© 1995 The Authors and Reece Winstone Archive & Publishing
No part of this book may be reproduced, copied or transmitted in any form or by graphic, mechanical or electronic
means or stored in any information storage or retrieval system without the written permission of the publisher.

Origination by the Publisher & Create Publishing Services Ltd
Printed by The Bath Press

Foreword

Hindsight can easily befuddle issues, but as seen from the mid '90's this period seemed to offer so much promise. First, there was the hope that issues of land transport could cease to be the juggernaut before whose needs all must be sacrificed. The Avon County Council Land Use Transportation Study (LUTS), based on work started by the City and County of Bristol and published in 1975, set the tenor for the late 1970's : limitations on car-use were accepted as desirable, road schemes (particularly the Inner Circuit Road) were pruned back and the positive role of public transport was acknowledged. Second, the general quality of the built environment of the city and its suburbs was becoming much more widely appreciated and understood. The exhibition at the City Museum and Art Gallery to mark European Heritage Year in 1975 and its accompanying booklet by Clare Crick, *The Victorian Buildings of Bristol*, was but one of the studies that drew attention to aspects which had been little regarded hitherto. Third, the campaign of archaeological excavations and fieldwork instigated by the City Museum and Art Gallery had demonstrated conclusively that the archaeology of the centre of the city had not been totally eradicated by later cellarage and services but survived well enough to be recorded and interpreted using modern archaeological techniques. Moreover, in a tight-knit built-up area which had been developed in and from the Middle Ages, later buildings had been developed within the physical constraints of their sites and had made creative use of these limitations. In doing so, substantial parts of earlier standing structures were likely to be reused and to survive encased in later work. Such survivals could be predicted and sought out, but were terribly vulnerable to the kind of comprehensive redevelopment that might be agreed for a relatively small (in modern terms) urban site. And so, fourth, there was an awareness, perhaps not as apparent as it should have been, that the renewal of the quality of city life was a far more subtle process demanding understanding of the interdependence of the structures that made up the fabric of the City.

The superb collection of photographs in this book might suggest this view to be hopelessly optimistic. The effects of the gathering pace of closure of so many of the traditional industrial and commercial activities in the centre of the city, typified by the closure of the City Docks for most commercial use, is eloquently documented. Would the imagination and resources for redevelopment, particularly the rehabilitation of so many key historic areas, be forthcoming? Yet there were signs that things could change. The redevelopment of St Bartholomew's Hospital at the foot of Christmas Steps showed that it was possible to conserve and enhance important elements of the townscape - not just the well-known fish-and-chip shop and newsagents, but other hidden structures, even parts of the Norman hallhouse, reused in succession as a home for the medieval hospital, Bristol Grammar School, Queen Elizabeth's Hospital and model dwellings for the industrial classes. The purchase of four cranes on Prince's Wharf by a group of private citizens (City Docks Ventures Ltd, CDV) showed that private, small-scale intervention could secure the future of distinctive landmarks.

Hindsight may be a luxury, but through the amazing series of books of which this is the latest, published by the Winstones, father and son, Bristolians have a rich source of images to enjoy and think upon.

David Dawson, curator Somerset County Museum, Taunton
formerly curator in archaeology, Bristol Museum

Introduction

The 1994 exhibition and biography *Rambles... from the Darkroom* will have put Reece's work in a different light for many readers, widening his persona into that of freelance photographer, rather than that of recorder or documentary photographer and collector. The author had the pleasure of being reminded once again, by testimonials in the visitors' book, of his father's energy, efficiency, business acumen and tenacity. Such was the man and his involvement with 'things Bristol'.

In the present volume the accent changes again. In 1974 Reece chose to cease his one-man recording of Bristol and to concentrate on publishing. He was then sixty-five and his last black-and-white coverage was of the return to Bristol in 1970 of the SS *Great Britain*.[1] This project was dear to Reece as encapsulating that which might have been achieved by the City, had authority grasped the nettle sooner. In the event it was not until 1976 (**83**) that official support came.

After this Reece filled his camera with colour transparency film, even buying his first 35mm camera, and made slides of a more personal record, including Bristol and beyond. There are more than 2,000 of them and selecting from them has been, on occasion, an overwhelming experience. These, coupled with the author's own shots in both colour and black-and-white, made it essential to include at least some colour printing. That might also have been a feature of volume 38, *Bristol As It Was 1963-75*, had funds allowed. Accordingly, a number of Reece's biographical colour shots pre-1976 have been included in this volume, and one essential colour record shot of St Augustine's Parade, taken by a contributor, and one or two others from slides. Old acquaintances figure, mostly taken within the period, each having made a great impact in their field. Included are Miss Elizabeth Ralph, former city archivist; the late David Verey, author of the *Buildings of England* series for Gloucestershire; Angus Buchanan, industrial archaeologist; the late Dorothy Vinter, local historian; and the late John Totterdill, Mancunian *emigre* and architect-planner.

Reece indulged himself too in photographing shops which sold his books, perhaps for his own eyes alone, but twenty years on these speak loudly of changes at the local newsagent, of the place of the small private bookseller in town and suburb and the appearance of shopfronts. There is a lack of clutter, no vandal-proofing and perhaps more gay colours than are presently fashionable.

The author's viewpoint with a camera is more specifically angled. One is tempted to suggest that it sought places where vision was required. The cameras he used were an Olympus OM1 with normal lens and, on occasion, Reece's wide angle Envoy 120, which by then had been handed down. The author had close contact with the city following a move into Kingsdown in 1974, where he remained well beyond the period of the volume. This bonding was effectively completed when in 1977, during convalescence, he decided he should start a full-time architect's practice.[2] By 1979 a small lettable space was taken in King Street, a listed building conversion well before its time. The same year he was brought up short with the unpalatable fact that all this time, through the sixties and seventies, the local conservation lobby for all its apparent professionalism had been blinkered and could miss a case such as the proposed demolition of 10 Lower Park Row (**223**). This single event did much to set the tone for the author's succeeding decade and the current one also.

An outline of conservation in Bristol was given in volume 38. An extension of this is best left for a future volume which can review the still current Joint Conservation Programme and ask why such little actual conservation was achieved. Although an account of 10 Lower Park Row appeared in *Bristol & Avon Archaeology 1983*, several points should be stressed. A demolition application was made without internal examination of a listed building. Then certain local conservation groups gave the building short shrift for fear it might somehow jeopardise the refurbishment of Georgian Lodge Street, itself scheduled to have Georgian rooms cut about. The author won the argument only because he out-manoeuvred the opposition. Armed with only the slightest of introductions to the adjoining owner, the late Eric Gadd, better known as 'Captain Courage', the author asked on the doorstep if he would give away a three-foot strip of his already small garden to provide access to the 5-bay front of No. 10 in order to save the building. To his amazement Eric agreed. To the credit of the planning authority the City Council grasped both the opportunity and the added grant offered by HBC as part of the Programme package, and the application to demolish was withdrawn. The case led to the setting up of the Avon branch of the SPAB in 1982, for the Society was drawn in on the subsequent matter of the damaging conversion scheme. It also became apparent in the years to follow that numerous professional agents, often the most distinguished, showed themselves to be nothing of the kind, when seen at public inquiries. There was also a continuing stream of damaging planning and listed building applications, which were frequently approved, against reasoned advices from the national amenity societies. This situation was then often compounded by the giving of so-called conservation awards, when in fact an inside knowledge of buildings and building works showed many to have been actively damaged in rehabilitation.

This then was the author's motivation for many photographs. A geographer, Mike Crang, at the University of Durham, reminded us of the importance of setting out the photographer's agenda in a paper on *Envisioning Urban Histories* (forthcoming) and using as his model Reece's published oeuvre. He refers to the process as 'salvage photography' and concludes that a photographer's activity should be granted sequential presentation to reduce distortion. The limitations of the collecting process and our ideas of chronology militate against this, but the criticism has been borne in mind. A sequential grouping of photographs has been followed for each year, usually in the order of gardens, churches, housing, public buildings, industry, docks and transport.

Reece's shots may be readily identified by the added dimension of exact time of day and date. Some may notice a greater partiality towards buildings in this volume given the absence of Reece's fuller recording, in particular his capture of streetscape. That shortcoming is the author's, who took all the photographs not covered either by Reece's timed entries or those listed below. Efforts have been made to correct this with numerous forays into the albums of colleagues, such that in all many thousands of pictures have been considered. Since colleagues' agendas are known to a degree it is worth attempting a paraphrase of them here, in acknowledging their contributions and copyright: Avon County Council, Ms Mary Stacey, conservation officer, who located the colour slides of her predecessors, including Michael Dawson (reunited here with his article), Jenny Birkett, James Edgar, Rob Iles and Chris Smith, (none expressly identified) taken in order to build the County's planning resource, nos. 2-9, 35, 55, 58, 59, 91, 94, 114, 130, 131, 136, 137, 164, 198, 202, 205, 255-7, 266, 267, 291; Chris Bocci, architect, who gave assistance with old photographs of the site of his new police station in Trinity Road, 248; Dr James Briggs, Civic Society committee member and amateur recorder of modern Bristol much in Reece's manner, generously opened his medical cabinet of his own and others' colour slides, 1, 20, 29, 30, 138, including one by the late John

Totterdill, appearing here for the first time, 259; Bristol Museums, 95, 96; British Aerospace, D J Charlton, 68; John Bryant, archaeologist and recorder of Bristol buildings for Bristol Museums, who provided a shot to the Victorian Society, 248; Jerry Cottignies AIBP provides a shot commissioned by Mike Jenner for his book *Bristol: an architectural history*, on his large format camera, 172; Damian Gillie, freelance, 292; Hunting Aerofilms Ltd, cover; Adrian Jones, another local architect who also made forays with a 35mm camera, with an equally specific point to argue at the time - that of encouraging reuse of historic buildings, especially in the Docks, and one of the main organisers of *20 Ideas for Bristol*, 34, 45, 57, 71-5, 78-81, 84, 85, 108, 147, 305; David Morgan, Bristolian and amateur with a love of cameras, if in need of a subject here finds one with his personal coverage of the Queen's Jubilee on professional filmstock loaded in a Nikon, 87, 97, 98, 102-7; Geoff Roberts, Somerset County photographer who, with the late Bob Rowe (also of the Wyvern Photographic Society), was commissioned to cover the Clifton Fayre also using Nikon cameras and an audio-visual record, 188, 191; Jem Southam, professional freelance working from Bristol at the time with a large format camera and notably in his fine book jointly with John Lord on the landscape of *The Floating Harbour*, 210, 213, 215, 270; John Trelawny-Ross, architect and amateur, who was employed by the City Council Urban Design Section (the section charged with the Joint Conservation Programme) at the time - the work of his large format camera, often in place early on a weekend, figures prominently in *Bristol: an architectural history* and appears here again with Michael Jenner's kind agreement, 21, 39, 47, 48, 50, 51, 86, 118, 261; and finally Brian Tuff ARPS, head of photography at Brunel College, producing for his own purposes a fine print of Gas Ferry Road, perhaps unaware of the plight of the thoroughfare, endpaper.

Thanks are also due to others who have most kindly responded to the author's enquiries including L Neath of Braby Silos; David Eveleigh, curator at Blaise Castle House Museum; staff at the Bristol Record Office; Peter Fulwood, local TV cameraman, for identifying staff members; landlord and customers of The Crown PH, Hambrook; Jeremy Johnson-Marshall, architect of the Dome; Andy King, assistant curator Bristol Industrial Museum; Ivor Morris, former Lord Mayor's coachman; Michael Pascoe for help with Clifton Fayre; Bill Pickard for permission to include his poem *Photographic Memory*; Miss Elizabeth Ralph for B&GAS members' names; Michael Tozer for all commercial vehicle conundrums; Brian Rome for research on the Barrow Road viaduct; and Methuen, Reed Corporation, publishers of *John Betjeman Letters*, compiled by Candida Lycett Green, for permission to quote Betjeman on St Mary-le-Port. We are grateful to Gordon Young at Create Publishing Services for remaining unruffled throughout and for liaison with staff at The Bath Press. Cotters Photography printed black-and-white and colour negative film and Dr Steve Berger unjammed our electronic origination!

The bonus of having David Dawson's foreword returns to Reece's practice of inviting the views of someone intimately connected with events in the period. David is unusual for being an archaeologist with an interest and eye for standing buildings. Bristol's loss is Taunton's gain as is clear to the visitor to Taunton Castle. Michael Dawson (no relation), another principal officer, most kindly agreed to write about the influence of the County of Avon. It was felt that this was both timely and overdue, and Mike also has useful reminders for his planning successors in the new authorities. With pressures to conurbate more densely, reorganisation will have far reaching consequences, and will determine how responsibilities are taken, or not, for historic areas in particular. The indicators are not encouraging. To all these, to the subscribers and to Rosie for editing, my thanks are due.

The Chronology, which prefaces each year, is based on Reece's Changes in the Face of Bristol newssheets and has been expanded from a variety of sources, including the following publications: *Avon Conservation News*; Avon Gardens Trust newsletters; *20 Ideas for Bristol* catalogues; CPAB minutes 1976-80; City of Bristol monthly *News*. Those buildings that have received grant aid from the Joint Conservation Programme are identified in bold type. Readers may wish to note that it is a condition of grant that such buildings may be visited by appointment. It remains to apologise in advance for any inadvertent errors in the telling of events unfolding. Efforts have always been made to check facts, but some errors are inevitable where numerous discrete events overlay others. Readers are reminded that the Archive can make available (subject to copyright) copies of published photographs.

John Winstone
Ilex House, Churchill
September 1995

Footnotes

1: The author well remembers the acquisition in 1966 of a shot taken in 1950 by Olin Pettingell, a Walt Disney producer, of 'The Ship' as she was referred to, demasted in the Falklands' Sparrow Cove (long before the Cove grew another history), and which appeared in *Bristol's Earliest Photographs*. The author, interested in ships and then a student, on seeing the photograph had the romantic idea of returning her to Bristol, but had best keep quiet! A similar idea of rescuing the beached trow *Jonadab* at Lydney in 1981, at first appeared so easy after the return of SS *Great Britain*, despite others having failed to save the trow *Safety* beached adjacent B Bond in the early 70's, but proved impossible without naval know-how.

2: This brought forth the rejoinder from Dorothy that it was 1936 all over again, when Frank (as RW then was), made a similar decision to move from part-time to full-time photography.

The County of Avon 1974-1996 by Michael Dawson

former Divisional Planning Officer responsible for Landscape & Conservation in Avon County Council and currently Assistant County Planning Officer, Surrey County Council

Bristol had had just one council responsible for its local government for 800 years. At midnight on 1 April 1974 this state of affairs changed. The new administrative County of Avon was brought into being and with it two tiers of local government - Bristol City Council and the new Avon County Council.

The new arrangements were part of a nationwide reform of local government, which had been initiated by the Prime Minister, the late Harold Wilson, in the 1960's, and pushed through by the succeeding Heath government in the early 1970's.[1] The new system had been fiercely resisted by the outgoing City Council, not least because of worries about the likely political complexion of the new County Council. However, the new arrangements would also split local government functions in the City for the first time - with the County Council looking after Education, Social Services, Highways & Transportation and Strategic Planning, while Local Planning, Housing and Environmental Health would remain with the City Council.

Despite this hostility, for many people there was much logic in uniting the City with its hinterland. In particular, this was designed to overcome the deep divisions and suspicions which had been rife between the City Council and the surrounding Somerset and Gloucestershire County Councils. A particular worry of the two County Councils had been the continuing growth of the City, which had led to a succession of City boundary extensions encompassing new housing areas, and which constantly threatened to overflow into the strongly defended Green Belt.

The establishment of the new County was also a recognition that the Avon area had always been, in many ways, a natural geographical, social and economic entity. Planning studies of the Avon area dated back to the Patrick Abercrombie 1930 Bristol & Bath Regional Planning Scheme.[2] In the 1960's the regional strategy for the South West had recognised a Bristol-Severnside Sub-Regional Division with boundaries very similar to Avon County.[3] The strategy gave rise to a separate study of the Avon area, 'The Severnside Feasibility Study' published in 1971, which highlighted the problems outlined above.[4]

The new Avon County Council was regarded with mixed feelings by local conservation groups. The scale of demolition and change in Bristol in the preceding 25 years had been greater even than that wrought during the war years. These changes are graphically and fully portrayed in previous volumes in this series. Nevertheless, many local people regarded the local government reorganisation with suspicion. Why was it necessary to have two councils, where one had sufficed before? Would this not lead to a growth in bureaucracy? How could councillors hailing from Bath and Weston-super-Mare take decisions affecting Bristol? Would they not have little interest in and less knowledge of Bristol's needs?

The omens for a change of approach indeed were not reassuring at first. In the early months of 1974 many of the Councillors and Highways staff from Bristol City Council House moved the mile across the City centre to the County Council's Avon House headquarters at St James' Barton. By July 1975 the new County Council had already spent £2.5m on land acquisition and demolition of houses at Totterdown for the much reviled Outer Circuit Road. This scheme, adopted in the 1966 Bristol Development Plan by the previous City Council, had been inherited by the County Council,

(2) *c.*1979: **Wells Road** looking north across the waste of Totterdown

(3) *c.*1976: **Oxford Street, Totterdown** Nos 64-69 before clearance of the south side

(4) *c.*1976: **Kilkenny Bay, Portishead** 'keep unspoiled the coastline'

(5) *c.*1977: **Tortworth**, early recognition of the importance of the house and park, before its tragic fire and erosion of the setting

who then budgeted a further £14m for a continuation of the destruction.

Howard Stutchbury, newly appointed as County Planning Officer, previously had been City Architect and Planning Officer of Bath. He had attracted huge opposition for his role in the rapid changes to that City's Georgian heritage. This had been portrayed in the emotively titled *The Sack of Bath*. [5] He now had the task of shaping a strategic approach to dealing with the continuing massive local growth in population and traffic, and demands for housing, jobs, leisure and road space. The Structure Plan for Avon was to be the vehicle for reconciling these demands with the need to conserve the historic cities of Bristol and Bath, resist development in the surrounding Green Belt, and keep unspoiled the coastline, internationally important for its wildlife, and the outstanding natural beauty of the Mendips and Cotswolds.[6]

The Avon County Planning Department which was responsible for preparing the Structure Plan started to form a conservation team in 1975. The first job of the team was to begin the systematic assembly of data on the County's heritage of buildings, archaeology, parks, landscape and wildlife. Also begun was an assessment of the conservation issues facing this heritage and of ways of dealing with these issues, the first time that such an evaluation of the local heritage had been undertaken.[7]

These fledgling efforts, begun in 1976, to rapidly assess features of conservation value in the County were to lead, during the succeeding 20 years, to the development of comprehensive, detailed and computerised conservation records for the whole County. The importance of these detailed records cannot be over-estimated. In many cases, these records form the only source of information available to planners. Without such records there can be no systematic way in which decisions on planning applications can take account of features of conservation importance. The County Conservation Team's efforts over these years led to a 50% growth in the number of listed buildings in the County, while records of important archaeological and wildlife sites increased by a staggering 500%.

Another priority of County Council work during this period, with considerable significance for the future, was the development of environmental education. Creation of the Bristol Urban Studies Centre in All Saints' Church, Corn Street, stimulated a host of new conservation-focused activities for school children in central Bristol. At the same time, the County Council's innovative Resources for Learning Development Unit, within a remarkably short period, had published some very stylish and usable educational resource packs covering a variety of topics, including medieval Bristol and the City Docks.

Building on the huge growth of public concern for conservation in the late 1960's and 1970's, the County Conservation Team put effort into developing links with voluntary conservation organisations, stimulating local activity and providing help and support. The publication of *Avon Conservation News* provided a focus for this.[8] Other efforts gave rise to the organisation of a host of Government-funded environmental conservation schemes for the unemployed. These rapidly became the largest group of such organisations in the West of England. This was paralleled by the birth of a number of new Countywide environmental charities - including Avon Wildlife Trust (**218**) (now the Wildlife Trust for Bristol, Bath & Avon), Avon Industrial Buildings Trust, Avon Farming & Wildlife Advisory Group and Avon Gardens Trust.

A number of Bristol amenity societies successfully influenced policy developments and decisions on individual planning applications, by the County and City Councils, during the 1970's - and two in particular, the Bristol Visual & Environmental Group and the Bristol Civic Society. BVEG, led by the indomitable Dorothy Brown, formed a buildings preservation trust which became very active in the efforts to restore buildings in Old Market (**138, 139**), following publication in 1979 of the study of Old Market, commissioned by the City Council and Bristol Municipal Charities.[9] The Civic Society was also increasingly involved in practical conservation activities. Its Tree Appeal, launched in 1973, slowly transformed much of central Bristol (**18**), including the docks. They cleared eyesores in the newly designated Redcliff Conservation Area, and in 1980 published *The Fight for Bristol*.[10] This provided a valuable retrospective of the post-war conservation campaigns. The Brunel Engineering Heritage Trust, inaugurated in 1979, was set up to restore Brunel's Old Temple Meads Station. In 1980 the building was upgraded by the Secretary of State to Grade I, and British Rail was persuaded to begin making it weathertight.[11]

This period also saw environmental themes achieving even greater media attention. There was a succession of high profile national events: Plant a Tree in '73, European Architectural Heritage Year 1975, Heritage Education Year 1977, 1979 - The Year of the Garden, The Countryside in 1970 and 1980. These were paralleled by a number of locally important events. Not least of these were the three highly influential and popular *20 Ideas for Bristol* exhibitions held in 1975, 1976 and 1980 (**75, 303**).

The, by now, unstoppable growth of public interest in conservation was also being reflected in the actions of Bristol City Council. Perhaps the most significant change had been the appointment, in 1975, of Jim Preston as the first City Planning Officer. Prior to that, town planning in Bristol had been under the direction of the City Engineer. Now planning and conservation would have their own remit, separate from highway engineering. Sadly, Mr Preston died in 1977, but he had formed the City Council's own Conservation Team, led initially by Graham Field. With the gaining of priority town status from the Secretary of State in 1976, significant amounts of grant aid for building conservation work became available for the first time, from the City and from the Government's

(6) 1975: **Backwell Quarry**, looking north-west to Tickenham Hill distant

(7) 1977: **Upton Cheyney** The ravages of Dutch Elm disease

(8) undated: **Narrow Quay** Environmental education in the City Docks

(9) *c.*1980: **Kelston** Drystone walling in white lias with MSC labour

Historic Buildings Council, under a Joint Conservation Programme. The City Council established a Conservation Advisory Panel in 1977, whose first chairman was the Civic Society's Richard Flowerdew. Membership of the Panel included some of the hitherto most outspoken critics of the City's conservation record. In the same year a new statutory list of historic buildings for Bristol was issued by the Secretary of State. This increased the number listed by 40% and added 1,000 buildings in the central area alone.

It was also in 1977 that the County and City Councils set up a joint study team for the City Docks. It is hard now to recall that the City Council in the 1960's had proposed the closure of the City Docks, and partial infilling of the harbour, due to the enormous costs of upkeep. Unparalleled local opposition had forced a change of mind [**38/308**], and the bill to close the Docks was withdrawn in 1976. Not even the bringing back to Bristol of the SS *Great Britain* in 1970 had been entirely welcomed by the City Council, until millionaire Jack Hayward stepped in to support the project (**83**).

New policies began to emerge in 1978, to be followed by numerous developments. The Industrial Museum was opened in M Shed, shortly to be followed by the National Lifeboat Museum, while BIAS was asked to prepare a report on the future of Underfall Yard. St Augustine's Reach, Baltic Wharf and Hotwell Dock were redeveloped with leisure facilities and housing. New pubs, restaurants and recreational boats were soon to be seen everywhere, and the holding of the first World Wine Festival in 1978 seemed to encapsulate this new era. The City Docks were designated a conservation area in 1979 and Bristol won a Europa Nostra Award for the City Docks in 1984.

The County Council published its Bristol Land Use Transportation Study (LUTS) in 1975.[12] This demonstrated the unacceptable cost in both financial and conservation terms of attempting to provide roads to cater for the forecast growth in traffic. It proposed draconian measures to reduce traffic flows into the City Centre, including the use of tolls. Although most of the proposals were not implemented at this point, the study did lead to a change of approach towards highway planning. Most significantly, in Bristol, it led to the abandonment by the County Council in 1977 of the plans for the Outer Circuit Road. This lifted the blight on what remained of properties along the line of the proposed road in Totterdown, Bedminster, Clifton and Montpelier. It allowed conservation work to be begun on affected derelict and disused buildings. New housing was eventually built on the devastated hillsides above the Three Lamps Junction. In due course the County Council also changed its mind about diverting traffic away from Queen Square and routeing it along The Grove and across Narrow Quay to Canon's Marsh.

The separation of local government functions between the County and City Councils probably did help to concentrate the City Council's attention on conserving its historic areas. The County Council was in a good position to direct strategic growth away from Bristol centre and to the developing areas on the northern edge of Bristol - superstores at Cribbs Causeway, offices at Aztec West and housing at Patchway and Stoke Gifford, with the Avon Ring Road around the east of Kingswood to divert through traffic away from the City. This approach was linked with policies to limit the amount of new offices in the central area and, where appropriate, to require office development to conserve listed buildings and conservation areas.

These policies, contained in the Avon Structure Plan, were by no means universally welcomed at the time. The Civic Society and many groups and individuals living in north Bristol were alarmed at the prospect of pulling back the Green Belt boundaries to the M4 and M5 lines. A particular concern was the preservation of Green Areas on either side of the M32, along this most important of entries to the City. South of the City there was doubt about the wisdom of encouraging residential development along the coast - particularly at Clevedon and Weston-super-Mare. Moreover, many people felt that the new office policies were too late and that they would do little more than promote the retention of facades in the Bristol conservation areas. Some of these concerns have been shown to have some substance, which successive reviews of the Structure Plan have sought to address.

Ironically, another Conservative Government twenty years on has decided to put the local government clock back. From midnight on 1st April 1996 Avon County will become an historical footnote. Time will tell whether the untried voluntary arrangements for strategic planning, to be set up on the demise of the County Council, will work to prevent battles once again between the City of Bristol and the surrounding rural areas.

Footnotes

1 The Royal Commission on Local Government in England, under the Chairmanship of Lord Redcliffe Maud, reported in 1969, recommending the formation of a new County of Avon. The new County was created by the Local Government Act 1972.

2 ' Bristol & Bath Regional Planning Scheme', Abercombie, P & Bruton, BG, 1930.

3 'A Region with a Future: A Draft Strategy for the South West', South West Economic Planning Council, 1967.

4 'Severnside: A Feasibility Study', Central Unit for Environmental Planning, 1971.

5 *The Sack of Bath*, Ferguson, A, 1973. Republished in 1989 as *The Sack of Bath - and After* with an added chapter by Tim Mowl covering the period 1973-1989.

6 The Avon County Structure Plan has a chequered history. It was submitted to the Secretary of State in 1980. Following a change of political control on the County Council it was withdrawn in 1981, and was resubmitted after redrafting in 1982. The Plan was approved in 1985, after a public inquiry. Avon thus had the dubious distinction of being the last County Council to bring a Structure Plan into operation.

7 A number of situation reports were produced as background to the Avon Structure Plan. These included 'Countryside Studies 2', 'Historic Environment', and 'Environmental Pollution and Derelict Land', all 1978.

8 *Avon Conservation News* first appeared in Feb. 1977 and the last issue was No. 34, published in Jan. 1993. With its great variety of conservation topics, it gained a wide local following. Significant were Understanding Buildings July '77 - May '79; Historic Landscapes July '79 - Jan. '81; the debate provoked by the issues on facadism Aug. '86 & Feb. '87.

9 'Old Market Conservation Study', Bristol City Council & HBC, 1979.

10 *The Fight for Bristol*, eds Priest, G and Cobb, P, 1980.

11 A grant application was turned down on the author's recommendation in the late '80's and a damaging proposal to convert Brunel's Engine Shed and drawing office was opposed by the Victorian Society in 1991 without much success. EH subsequently gave grant for repairs to the roof and facade of the Train Shed.

12 'Bristol Land Use Transportation Study', Avon County Council, 1975.

(10) 3.30pm 3 May 1979: Hyland Grove An HTV camera crew of 5 film RW. L to R: Ken Alderman, sound recordist; clapper loader; David Hillier, cameraman; unknown; and Brent Sadler, reporter.

(11) 6.15pm 9 January 1980: Narrow Quay A BBC camera crew of 3 film RW. L to R: Rik Calder, cameraman; John Norman, reporter; Ron Dayben, sound recordist.

(12) 6.15pm 15 April 1970: Advisory Committee on Bristol History meeting in the Director's Office, Bristol Museum & Art Gallery, Queen's Road, with RW's recent vol. 14 on the table. L to R: Max Hebditch, curator of social history, now Director, Museum of London; John Totterdill; Dr Angus Buchanan; Mr Cleeve; Mrs Dorothy Vinter; Alan Warhurst, director; and Mr Davis.

(13) 11.50am 17 July `76: B&GAS meeting at Hailes Abbey L to R: Miss Elizabeth Ralph, secretary and former Bristol City Archivist; David Verey, author of *Buildings of England* for Glos.; C Roy Hudleston, president; Mrs E Clifford, archaeologist; and Col. AB Lloyd Baker.

(14) 4.30pm 17 July `76: Tiverton RW and Dorothy show off RW's recent FRPS at a WCPF AGM.

(15) 10.30am 21 September 1975: College Road The Rt. Hon. the Lord Mayor of Bristol Councillor Hubert Williams driven by Ivor Morris, coachman, with footman dressed in informal uniform with cockade in top hats, with Badminton and Beaufort in harness. This landau, built in 1896 by J Fuller & Co. of St George's Road, was dispensed with in 1991 at the same time as the state coach and coachmen, save for very occasional appearances. It can be seen in the Industrial Museum.

(16) 1.50pm 31 August 1975: Canon's Marsh A bus rally with a backdrop of the tobacco bonds. Left to right: Bristol L5G chassis with Easton Coachworks (Lowestoft) body, built Dec.1949, LHY 976; Blue pre-war Bristol K5G with Bristol body, GHY 154?; Bristol L5G chassis with Eastern Coachworks body, KFM 767; Leyland Tiger chassis, JLJ 403.

(17) 2.45pm 26 May 1975: Kingsdown Parade The Street Fair in full swing. This had been inaugurated to celebrate the designation of the Kingsdown Conservation Area and continues most years. The author took a similar view the same afternoon [see **38/125** where it is mis-dated].

(18) 12.15pm 17 December 1975: Alma Vale Road Civic Society members plant a lime tree in memory of the late Phyllis Cox. A young bearded future Society chairman looks on right.

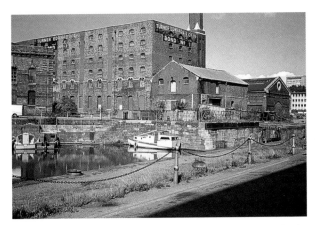

(19) 12.05pm 4 September 1975: Bathurst Parade in its post-commercial solitude. The basin railbridge has long gone [**18/114**]. Turner & Edwards No. 1 Bond, unlisted, formerly J Robinson & Son oil seed merchants, still with its boiler house but bereft of its lucam; all to go for gentrified houses (**306**).

(20) Possibly mid 1960's: Prince Street Bridge This industrial landscape shows the 4-ton cranes on Bathurst Wharf brought from Portishead post-war and Turner & Edwards No. 1 Bond with its lucam, full height stack (with lean) and pitched roof. Another stack rises right to J Warringer's warehouse.

(21) May 1971: St Augustine's Place, formerly the literal centre of the Tramways Centre, a grade II row of medieval houses in C19 dress, newly given the 'facelift' colour treatment, as it was called. One of the best schemes of Moxley, Jenner & Ptrs. Shortlived however and the row largely ruined in redevelopment, with the benefit of grant aid. The vestigial, but all important timber frames were lost. The fine 'phone, stamp and post box, left, went to West Som. railway!

(22) 10.30am 12 August 1977: Kingsmead Bookshop Early morning in Clevedon at a branch of a Bath bookshop, now closed.

(26) 4.30pm 20 May 1975: Temple Gate 'The fastest book lorry in the west' was RW's description of his Renault 5, here delivering to WHSmith wholesale - a veritable grotto of newsprint, changing daily. Now due for redevelopment.

(23) 11.20am 25 March 1977: North Street, Bedminster O Davies/Bellamy newsagent, another outlet for RW books.

(27) 9.30am 2 March 1971: Boots, Broadmead Fashionable Ms Wendy Jacobs arranges 11 RW titles on pegboard.

(24) 11.20am 10 August 1977: Winterstoke Road, Ashton Alan Roberts, with Brecknell Dolman's locally made cigarette machine prominent. He alone on this page now stocks RW books, save for WHSmith's, but only in The Galleries, Broadmead.

(28) 11.30am 9 March 1976: Queen's Road Showcase outside Daniel's school outfitters showing 14 RW titles.

(25) 12.40pm 10 August 1977: Wells Road Next after Alan Roberts that day was Knowle Post Office, adjacent Broadway shopping centre. RW's Renault 5 with advertising on removable cards in the side windows.

(29) Mid 1960's: Looking south along Stapleton Road at the Muller Road junction. The railway viaduct before demolition and now the site of Junction 2 on M32.

(30) 23 July 1974: Grosvenor Road Site of the St Paul's riots, looking north. The right-hand row, 1900's and *c.*1840, all of 300 metres long, is boarded up prior to demolition for housing, which was set back.

(31) July 1975: Totterdown Looking due south from the footbridge; Albert Road off left. A row of 3 houses, middle distance right, clung on until the bitter end. A fashion for blue-painted stucco is now appearing on houses, visible in the original transparency.

(32) 4.45pm 30 August 1975: Withywood, Bishopsworth and Hartcliffe from Dundry Wills Hartcliffe, right, and CEGB Bedminster Down, the 2 great post-war purpose-built Bristol buildings, are both now rudderless.

(33) 3.15pm 17 January 1975: The high rise buildings above Perry Road Almost uniformly undistinguished, they were permitted without a high rise policy plan. Compare with 1963 [**38/3**], 1957 [**37/254**] and 1920 [**17/57**].

(34) Late 1977: The Junction Locks and Hotwells Dock from Underfall Yard. The Hydraulic Engine House has been fired and a c.1840 row in Hotwell Road awaits demolition for road widening as a condition of development of the old Dock

(35) 1974: Portbury, the new M5 crossing and Junction 19. This and the West Dock pretty well did for Court House Farm, centre. Its pond, true centre, is seen in the foreground of (**94**).

(36) July 1979: Looking south-east from the author's roof in Kingsdown Parade. The gas holders off Folly Lane, left of centre, demolished for St Philip's Causeway. Broadweir site, centre, expected to lose its small scale. See[**38/4**].

(37) Midsummer 1979: Hotwells from Church Lane Taken in connection with the housing competition on Baltic Wharf. A rearguard action was fought to keep the sand boats. The loss of Wills Raleigh Road, *so* Bedminster, then unsuspected.

1976

Conservation Issues

Ashton Court: demolition and revamp in progress

Hope Chapel: new use announced

Richmond Hill: demolition consent refused for Edgecombe Hall

Historic Buildings at Risk

42-62 York Road, Bedminster

Brunswick Square, south side

Lodge Street, north side

78-100 St Michael's Hill

Arno's Castle Gateway

36-40 Old Market Street

Host Street/Christmas Street corner

90-124 Lower Cheltenham Place

25-31 Cumberland Street

Temple Meads Old Station - fire officer declares it unfit

New building in progress

GPO in Telephone Avenue

Students' residences in Clifton Road

Millar House flats on site of St Andrew's Hall, Merchants Road, Clifton

January

Merchants Road: St Andrew's Hall dem.

68 & 69 Redcliff Street (building south of Edwards Ringer & Biggs) demolished

Winstone Court, 34-40 St Michael's Hill, started on site (named after Reece)

Concorde in service, on 21st, with simultaneous Anglo-French take-offs

Bus stops given double yellow lines

Domestic paper salvage collection discontinued

Britain applies for £1,000 million IMF loan

February

Bishop John Tinsley enthroned

King David Hotel, St Michael's Hill, closed

Radio Bristol broadcasts City Council meeting

Corn Street pedestrianised outside the Corn Exchange

Pedestrian bridge erected across Bond Street to link multi-storey car parks

Harold Wilson resigns as Prime Minister, North Sea oil exported

March

Easton Family Centre opens for parishes of St Lawrence, St Gabriel [**38/302**] & Holy Trinity

St Augustine's Parade: combined telephone, stamp machine and post box adjacent bus offices moved to East Somerset Railway Centre, Cranmore (**21**)

Holy Trinity, Clarence Road: last wedding

Houlton Street to East Street: Newfoundland Road demolition begun

City Docks: private Bill to close docks in 1980 withdrawn

April

Joint Conservation Programme (Historic Buildings Council, later English Heritage & City Council) set up by grant of 'priority town' status by Secretary of State

Whiteladies Road Conservation Area designated

Southmead Road roundabout reduced

Bristol City promoted to Division 1

Sunday mail collection discontinued

Civic Society tree appeal, then 2 or 3 years old, transforms the working character of Narrow Quay

James Callaghan succeeds Harold Wilson as Prime Minister

May

St Stephen's May Day 6am service reinstated at Reece's request (**46**) [**38/148**]

Concorde commences transatlantic service

June

Eastville Park: railway bridge abutments removed

Summerhill Road, St George: faceted milestone cleaned [**12/203**]

Talbot Road: east side of railway bridge widened

Windmill Hill City Farm formed as DIY community resource on derelict land

July

Charles Hill yard: last launch of a ship

Hotwells: footbridge across A4 at end of Granby Hill erected

Parson Street/Bedminster Road corner widened

White Tree Road: prefabs demolished

St George's Church, St George, demolished

25-31 Cumberland Street: Civic Society opposes dem. application with 'replicas rarely capture the feel of what has gone' and wins on appeal. In Jan. '77: 'The great problem is how to keep the buildings standing after the inquiry'. Later Council grants demolition consent

Post-LUTS - Civic Society maintains Avon County discard principle of reducing city centre traffic and also decries moving to back of pavement lighting standards in Whiteladies Road to safeguard vehicles!

August

Newfoundland Road closed for 3 months

Portway reopened following rock removal at Seawalls

Garlicks, established 1846 [**11/p9**], name disappears

Rupert Street, The Crown & Dove PH demolished.

September

City Road: third bus lane appears

Gloucester Road: Woolworths leave (see November, below)

Lower Castle Street footbridge erected

Rupert Street & Lewin's Mead footbridges erected

Highbury Chapel becomes Cotham Parish Church

Corn Street pedestrianisation completed

Area E (part), Nos 78-100 at top and bottom of St Michael's Hill, to come out of BRI precinct and Crown control after constant reminders that this is blighted, surplus to requirements. This had been established in 1958 but hitherto not enacted. All surplus land is still not released, 38 years later. Surely a record! [**38/p38**]

Cromwell Road, Scala Cinema site: Ombudsman finds against Council in not registering successive planning applications

October

Hicks Gate to Stockwood, new road being

made

Centenary of the University

Tower Hill: Prince of Wales PH demolished in preparation for office redevelopment (Castle Gate and Company House, formerly Rogers brewery)

Filton: St Stephen's Press becomes Leo supermarket

City creates post of Industrial Development Officer

November

20 Ideas for Bristol (actually 31) 2nd exhibition follows the July 1975 show and features an RNLI Museum; a treed amphitheatre on Canon's Marsh (cf. Lloyds 1990); Law Courts in Small Street PO (cf. 1993); Avon Walkway; Trim Track on The Downs; City Docks Information Centre - to mention those that were taken up - 6 compared with 1 the previous year

Newfoundland Road reopened - Hill, Dale and East Streets lost, Newfoundland Street widened

Jolly's and Rowe's announce closure in January

Gloucester Road: Woolworths site becomes Walton's supermarket

December

Redcliff Conservation Area designated

King's Cinema closes on 4th

Blaise Castle repairs estimated to cost £30,000

4 & 6 Park Street demolished by gas explosion and fire at 4.40am on 29th On 31st, No. 2 Park Street pulled down on safety grounds of threat to Park Street bridge

Captain Fred Hobart, Dockmaster, based at Underfall Yard, retires

(38) left - February 1976: The Promenade
Dutch Elm disease required these trees, and many others on Clifton Green, be felled.

(39) June 1976: St Mary-le-Port of local Pennant rubble, formerly plastered, shows 2 former roof profiles. Betjeman wrote to Alan Pryce-Jones about Anglo-Catholic practices, 17 April 1937: 'We must explore BRISTOL. There is a lot of LOW there. St Mary-le-Port is blackgown Calvinist. Alms are collected in a "decent basin"...Communion can be received standing...'

(40) February 1976: Emmanuel church, Guthrie Road John Norton's Geometric revival of 1865-9 before its nave and chancel were lost for sheltered housing, a reuse scheme that never worked well and left a landmark tower as if that were the criterion.

(41) August 76: St Werburgh's Park and Church was to be another casualty of redundancy and reuse. Here it casts its superior origins over a poor and proud early C20 suburb.

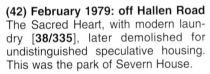

(42) February 1979: off Hallen Road
The Sacred Heart, with modern laundry [**38/335**], later demolished for undistinguished speculative housing. This was the park of Severn House.

(43) March 1979: off Hallen Road
Severn House, G Repton's *c.*1820 villa left in its last stages of deliberate decay by the developer of the flats, which have, as their prize, noisy M5.

(44) top - February 1976: The Fossway St James's Chapel of Ease, later Clifton Parish Hall, seen during demolition for speculative flats with a negative effect on the conservation area.

(45) 1976: Apsley Road, St John's Clifton by SJ Hicks, 1841. An undisciplined design by a local man for the Church Commissioners. Significantly in '88, its planted churchyard, a green lung in the conservation area, was lost.

(46) 3.00pm 21 June 1976: St Stephen's Avenue BBC *Points West* crew, with Graham Purchase exiting the tower vice of St Stephen's. RW had campaigned for the reinstatement of the tower-top service, and this might explain the BBC interest. Services were perhaps less easy after Ralph Edwards added a sound-exit lantern for the bells [**38/148**].

(47) left - June 1975: Hope Chapel Hill The Chapel founded in 1788, by Ladies Hope and Glenorchy, reordered 1838, here deplastered and its pediment simplified. A new use was announced in 1976.

(48, 49) left and below - 1976: Prince Street Nos 66-70, grade II, were threatened with demolition for a projected vehicular crossing of St Augustine's Reach. Last vestiges of the Bush warehouse railings, left, were removed without consent and delisted in the 1995 review. Meanwhile they had been replaced in replica to match those at No. 68. No.66 is a brick architecture, the more 'Bristol', and was over restored.

(50) May 1974: Royal York Crescent Nos 1-3 before their conversion in 1978 as retirement flats by a housing association. Eugenie House, as the end-piece is now called, takes its name from Eugenia de Montijo who was schooled here by the Misses Rogers as an eleven-year-old with her sister, later the Duchess of Alba. Eugenie became Empress of France and a confidante of Queen Victoria. The robbed and cemented-up shop beneath, right, was an elegant wine merchants in Neo-Classical style, Chas. Tovey & Co., at the time of the school [**40/92** & **39/62**].

(51) June 1976: King Street No. 6, refronted *c.*1720, before the brickwork was sand-blasted and damaged without consent *c.* 1992. Those to the right survive in their original, jettied form. The 1960's brick speculative office building towering behind is not an aberration of the camera but the product of a particularly damaging local practice of that time.

(52) February 1976: St Michael's Hill Winstone Court (as it was to be named, after RW) rises in a gap site. It appears the original staircase was sacrificed, but the general treatment was much appreciated. This shot shows how very invasive the hospital developments have been, with no noticeable improvement since the removal of Crown immunity.

(53) July 1976: **Ladies Mile** A self-sufficient sign-writer arrives on NHT 103F and paints 'Cycling Prohibited on the Downs'. Cyclebag and Sustrans' influence is yet to be felt on cycling provision.

(54) Late summer 1976: **King Square** Who remembers which particular event this was? *Pottery behind the Rainbow*, from Clifton and April Kerr, artist, have stalls and an inflatable awaits its blower.

(55) 1976: **Wells Road** opposite the Totterdown clearances. Possibly taken in connection with the County of Avon's campaign to preserve traditional shopfronts and illustrating well the process of forebuilding on front gardens, here at Nos 117 & 119 (then empty), of an unlisted brick terrace of *c.*1840. This was once a seemly street.

(56) May 1976: Dean Lane looking west from Dame Emily (Smythe) playground to Catherine Mead Street and Northfield House. The swimming pool, right, by CFW Dening, listed in 1995.

(57) 1976: Whiteladies Road Nos 59 & 61, former premises of Alexandra Co. [**39/164**], by '76 a discount store and Sunday papers were sold on the pavement. The Victorian Society objected to a proposal to demolish.

(58) below left - March 1976: Ashley Parade East side before demolition for realignment of Sevier and York Streets.

(59) below right - 1976: Portwall Lane GWR stabling for the Temple Meads Goods Depot, demolished for London Life offices, 1982.

(60) 12.30pm 24 November 1976: Goldney House This canal dates from 1758 when 3 other merchants were creating Gothick works, at Blaise, Warmley & Arno's Court. Intended to be closed on 3 sides, the right screen was lost. Goldney has been much put upon of late.

(61) Feb. 1977: Goldney canal fountain A Cornish engine raised water to the once plastered tower to serve the Georgian fountain. **(62)Taken by RW with (60) Goldney** Hercules before overdue repairs.

(63) 1976: Lodge Street on its knees. The reasons for the vacant parking lot in lieu of housing on the west side remain as unclear today as ever.

(64) 1976: off Marlborough Hill Cosey Cot, then blighted by infamous Area E hospital zoning; later repaired. The row below dem. for parking.

(65) 11.00am 25 June 1976: St Michael's Hill Winstone Court going up **(52)**.

(66 & 67) 1976: St Michael's Hill A deliberate attempt to get Nos 78-110 down. Crown immunity allowed the hospital authority to disregard listed building legislation. Local protesters painted them up and caused a furore. The buildings were offered HBC grant and saved only after telephone calls between the two Secretaries of State!

(68) 18 Feb. 1976: Gloucester Road North The Brabazon hangar occupied by the Concorde assembly line. The craftsmanship achieved in Concorde was the best coming out of Bristol at the time. The hangar, itself a great structure, remarkably is unlisted.

(69) 11.15am 22 August 1976: Henbury Road A London Transport Leyland Titan, KGU 284, passes a Bristol Omnibus Co. Bristol Bell chassis with Eastern coachwork, C1170 registration XAE 490H, at the old ford.

(70) May 1976: Hotwell Road MV *Balmoral* leaves the City Docks for an evening round trip down the Channel with a party, mostly of architects and engineers.

(71) 1976: Commercial Road The Holms Sand & Gravel Co. was another necessary removal if housing was to be proposed for the opposite side of Bathurst Basin (**20**).

(72) 1976 or '77: Hotwell Dock 2 centuries of usage: built *c.*1770. In 1983 the planners found this animated sandyard incompatible with housing.

(73) July 1976: Albion Dockyard Last out of Chas. Hill's yard, MV *Miranda Guinness*, bulk Guinness carrier, scrapped 1994. Closure of the yard in 1977 removed a trade that was free entertainment.

(74) 1976: Welsh Back Civic Society tree campaign in front of an unrestored MV *Blitz* in Eddie Shoestring country. Hideous 1970's office block, apologia Brygstowe, on the site of medieval Back Hall, which was excavated in 1995 [**27/62**, **32/123**].

(75) November 1976: City Art Gallery, Queen's Road Children and adults enjoy *20 Ideas for Bristol*, important for exhibiting the unsolicited thoughts of architects and designers, perhaps for the first time. Accessibility was a prominent theme, as was the City Docks.

(76) 1976: Hotwells To develop this site had long been an ambition of many; in *20 Ideas* it was seen as a waste land problem.

(77) May 1976: Leigh Woods 1867-1962 Portishead Branch line, to become Avon Walkway route in '77 with MSC labour; the City's *20 Ideas* proposal.

(78)1976: Bathurst Basin Looking east at Turner & Edwards Bond No. 1, built for J Robinson & Son, seed crushers, seen here with pitched roof and lucams removed. Unlisted, it was demolished for offices and houses and would have benefited from reuse. The Ostrich PH beyond, before alteration and extension.

(79) 1976: Queen Square Nos 43-47 Warriner's Bond, later 2nd home of the Arnolfini. Brick here signals the transformation of Georgian city to the Victorian industrial era and one C20 architects and planners could not stomach in 1991, for want of understanding, preferring instead cheap fakery.

(80) 1976: Hotwell Road No. 82 (right) had been identified by the Royal Commission on Historical Monuments as an early C18 3-bay house with winder stair opposite the stack (*Trinity Area of Frome*, Leech, 1981), but this did not result in its listing and went for nothing in refurbishment. The result actively damages the conservation area.

(81) below - 1976: MV *Harry Brown*, one of the sand boats, the last regular commercial users of the City Docks. A rearguard action was fought to keep them operational at Hotwells, but the pressure of development was such that conservation area considerations (and all that that entailed) would not prevail.

(82) & (83) right - 1976: Prince's Wharf & 7.15pm 4 May 1976: St Nicholas' Church Museum Meanwhile in the City Docks Braby Silos were still shipping out their silos from Ashton Gate works, here to go to ICI/EVC site at Barry, and the Rt. Hon. the Lord Mayor of Bristol, Councillor Hubert Williams, at last gives official support to the SS *Great Britain*.

(84) 1976: W Shed, Anchor Road In part 3rd home of the Arnolfini and now Watershed, following grant-aided reuse. No essential roof-top Armstrong-type travelling cranes survive in the City Docks [**18/4**, **37/214**].

(86) May 1976: Redcliff Backs
Buchanan's Warehouse. It's not difficult to imagine the waterfront arcade and quay unblocked for a harbourside walkway, or the added power of this most Bristol ensemble of Cattybrook brick rising sheer before the stack on the second block was demolished and Stoate's mill, beyond, was blitzed. The stack seen here was demolished, some lucams and conveyors (and much else) [**38/361**] removed in refurbishment. Stoate's was later rebuilt as flats set back a self-defeating 2 metres!

(85) 1976: Gas Ferry Road A listed group of walls, pavements, stack and gas buildings, before removal of the roof structure was unwisely acceded to. The gas lamp [**1/62**, **12/70**] long gone. Left, an early ferro-cement wharf by Mouchel-Hennebique.

(87) 1977: Downend
Silver Jubilee poster

Conservation Issues

Bristol City Council and Historic
Buildings Council Joint Conservation Programme commences.
Buildings so funded (and thus open to the public
on request) emboldened in the Chronology

Historic Buildings at Risk

St Stephen's, St John on the Wall*,
All Saints'*, Christ Church, St
George's Brandon Hill*, St
Michael's, St Thomas's* & St
James's*, under redundancy plans
* will be declared redundant

New Buildings in Progress

CEGB Bedminster Down
Cribbs Causeway: Hypermarket

January

Conservation Advisory Panel
  (CAP) set up
City Docks: Joint (Avon & Bristol)
  study team set up for local plan
  purposes & development princi-
  ples of 2 early release sites -
  Bathurst Basin & Hotwell Dock
Whiteladies Road: Demolition of
  Trinity Methodist for offices
  averted
Emmanuel Church, Guthrie Road:
  nave demolished for redevelop-
  ment as elderly persons' flats,
  with landmark tower retained
Southmead Rd: new police station
Thurston's Barton dem. [16/41]
Baltic Wharf: scheme for dinghy
  storage, caravans, slipway & club
  house proposed by South Bristol
  Technical College.
*Jimmy Carter inaugurated as 39th
  president of USA*

February

Sea Walls reopens for motor traffic
West Dock: 1st ship in; strikebound
  throughout the year
Avon Conservation News, 1st issue
Dutch Elm disease; appeal
  launched for Jubilee year.

March

New Statutory List of Buildings of
  Special Architectural and Historic

Interest signed: a 40% increase & adding 1,000 buildings in central area, despite many shortcomings

Trinity Road police station dem.

Frogmore Street reopens

Bristol Magpies formed to help the Museum & Art Gallery

Lulsgate airport: plans to expand to 4m passengers by 1990

Ashton Court: 1st phase nearing completion

April

Conservation Programme: Sec. of State grants Bristol Priority Town status enabling the 'ring of dereliction' in conservation areas to be grant funded

Redland Hill/Rd mini-roundabout set up

Fire largely destroys C16 Over Court in suspicious circumstances. Rescue bid fails to attract Housing Corporation funding, bringing to conclusion post-war boarding-up

Winstone Court, St Michael's Hill: 11 flats on bomb site opened by RW [**32/21**]

British Aerospace becomes public corporation

SPAB centenary; 'Repair not Restoration' booklet by local member

May

Horse-bus service from Centre to SS *Great Britain*

Speedway starts on the Rovers' ground

City churches: redundancy plans announced; opposed by CPAB in Oct. '78 on architectural & historic grounds.

St Mary-on-the-Quay: proposal to dem. chancel for new presbytery

Regent Street, Clifton: proposal to facade Nos 2-14

British Rail brings high speed train (HST) into service. Bristol/ Paddington claims long-run world record, 117 miles in 68.20 mins. 2x12 cly. Paxman Valenta diesel-electric 4,500 bhp

June

Steam car of 1875 [**7/146**] initially fails its MOT on brakes

Bristol Jubilee procession on 11th includes a float of Friese-Greene [**14/p33**] amongst 129 others

Jubilee scheme: Phoenician crowns back on 1912 Victoria Rms' masts

Wickham Glen becomes cul-de-sac both ends

Queen's Silver Jubilee on 7th

Royal Physicians' report on smoking; each cigarette takes 5 mins off a life

Brezhnev elected USSR president

July

St Bartholomew's Hospital (1240-1532, Grammar School 1532-1767, QEH 1768-1847) archaeology commences - 'best preserved parts of medieval town' - scheduling of Norman hall proposed in May

Broad Street/Tailors' Court: No. 43, C15 house above Beefeater restaurant empty & deteriorating

HBC offers £100,000 a year for 5 years, to be mainly spent in city centre for essential repairs to exteriors only -50% for charities, 25% for private owners, offer matched by City Council

Rupert Street to Lewin's Mead footbridge erected

XIV preparatory school in Druid Stoke Road closes

36 Corn Street: National Westminster Bank guts the interior

Alpha Rd, Southville, made one-way

August

Royal Portbury Dock opened by the Queen on 8th, followed by tour of displays on the Centre

Outer Circuit Road planned from Lawrence Hill to Three Lamps, Totterdown, abandoned

Ashton Court: two rooms fit for public use

SS *Great Britain* receives replica bridge

Park Street: skateboard demonstration by children

Jamaica Street/Hillgrove Street: Elim Pentecostal church hostel scheme reduced in scale

Civic lottery launch: £1k prize for 25p

Author commences his own practice

September

Kings Weston threatened with new police HQ development. Averted

Dolphin Street grassed over

Blackboy Hill: Connett's drapers close

Lower Castle St/Penn Street: Castlemead House high rise restarted by banks [**37/350**] after developer's liquidation in 1975

Stapleton Road: Pakistani restaurant explosion

Avon County finally agrees to scrap Outer Circuit road, including St Augustin''s Reach bridge

City Docks: Ferry service starts

Castle Park: to be completed to a Parks Dept layout

October

SS *Great Britain*: foremast stepped

Whitby Rd & Bloomfield Rd corner widened

Bath Road/West Town Lane carriageway dualling

November

Queen flies in Concorde

St Mary's, Tyndall's Park, sold to BBC as theatre store

Firemen's strike, army brought in

December

Hanham Methodist Church, Chapel Road dem. Replacement facade in '78 makes it unlistable

2,556 new houses built, many replacing prefabs, particularly the USA, APB & Aluminium - 7 types

City Docks: Council agrees to purchase Chas. Hill yard.

Lord Henley dies, supporter of opponents to Docks Bill in Lords.

BIAS celebrates 1st 10 years & reports on future of Underfall Yard

(88) 4.55pm 25 September 1977: Penpole Point, Kings Weston Evidence of Thos. Wright's work on the estate, before Vanbrugh, listed at the author's request.

(90) 1977: Goldney House, Clifton Hill Primary colours of a Bus Stop Tee shirt amongst tomatoes in the greenhouses.

(89) June 1977: Kings Weston Lane Vanbrugh's *c.*1720 Echo before grant-aided repairs. The statue of Venus is still missing.

(91) 1977: Hill End House, Henbury Little is known of this unliste house. Ca any reade help?

(92) 10 May 1977: Blaise Castle The first phase of Gothick at Blaise Castle, that of Thomas Farr, 1765. *'But now really - are there towers and long galleries?' 'By dozens'* the terrified Catherine Moreland was told in *Northanger Abbey*. There were never galleries here, and certainly not in 1977! In Victorian times there was a trophy room. Ingenious grant-aided repairs were at last carried out in 1980, which addressed the post-war neglect, but an ogee head of a Gothick fireplace surround was all the author recorded of internal features when assisting the architects.

(93) July 1977: Blaise Castle John Nash's 1806 Orangery for JS Harford on Blaise Castle Estate before lack of maintenance caused its temporary closure. Happily maintenance was carried out in 1994 and it is now a winter garden once again. Harford was president of the Archaeological Institute of Great Britain in 1851 and an enthusiast for Renaissance Rome. A small copy of Michelangelo's Medici Chapel sculpture is visible on the wall at the far end.

(94) *c.*1977: **Court House Farm, Easton-in-Gordano** looking south to the new M5 junction 19, seen in **(35)**.

(95) 8 August 1977: West Dock, Portbury HM the Queen shortly to name West Dock Royal Portbury, 5 years after commencement; the Rt. Hon. the Lord Mayor Cllr. Edward Wright at the microphone. The £1.3m Belgian gantry crane, designed for container handling, was sold off in a necessary move to the bulk cargo trade.

(96) 14 June 1976: West Dock Gordano shed was the first to be built. The massive crane tracks are visible right.

(97) June 1977: Frenchay Hill Post Office displays the monarch for the Silver Jubilee. A George V box inserted in a C19 6-pane shop window. The post office closed in the 80's with the retirement of the post-mistress, following a robbery.

(98) June 1977: The Crown PH, Hambrook Local residents line up in fancy dress.

From left Brian Cummins in mufti; in yellow behind Andrea Bristol in pushchair, Rene Breedon; Edna Holt right again; Fay Hutchinson with white Dutch hat with Penny; Rosemary Brookes as Britannia mouths to raised flag with Brenda Kislingbury behind; Jonathan Jackson with Nicholas Norris in ermine; Mrs Dench & Butler far right.

(99) 1977: Albemarle Row A Clifton Jubilee fair, which extended into Hope Chapel Hill and South Green Street. Albemarle Row, seen here with the road closed, built as lodgings for visitors to the spa, long ago lost its gardens opposite.

(100) & (101) 1977: South Green Street during the same Saturday Jubilee event as **(99)**, **(100)** rear of the school in front of Albemarle Row; **(101)** looking across open space to the Adam & Eve PH. The Hope Chapel schoolroom, left, was delisted following conversion. For the strange story of demolitions where the photographer stands see **[8/23]**.

(102) June 1977: West Mall A citizen's display equal to Thos. Foster's fine 1832 balconies with Greek Revival trim which have a lightness and showiness absent from the terrace itself.

(103) June 1977: Prince Street Bridge A very mixed team in PV *St Anne's* paddle past HMS *Venturer* moored outside the Bush warehouse.

(104) June 1977: Frenchay Common Mrs Barbara Scott, primary school teacher, hands out a picnic lunch to behatted pupils at Frenchay primary school. Hugo Morgan and Chris Lewis, centre.

(105) June 1977: Central Bristol A Hillman, AJY 167B, with spontaneous paint-job transports furniture to Knowle West?

(106) June 1977: The Mall, Clifton The now defunct Bristol Economic Building Society, apparently founded coincidentally in 1953, put on a somewhat bizarre choice of window display.

(107) 29 May 1977: Bathurst Wharf International power boat racing in the City Docks; the big boats are craned into the water. This spectacular was discontinued after fatalities.

(108) 1976: The Soft Map of Bristol This significant piece of 3-dimensional embroidery, some 12 feet long, by Libby Lee & Carol Dymond was based around the River Avon and its opportunities for new transport routes. It was displayed at *20 Ideas* and elsewhere. The mouth of the Avon is at the bottom; the Suspension Bridge is visible at $1/3$ length.

(109) 6.45pm 23 Feb. 1977: King Street Acker Bilk was shortly to be televised (pre-micro chips) in the newly pedestrianised street.

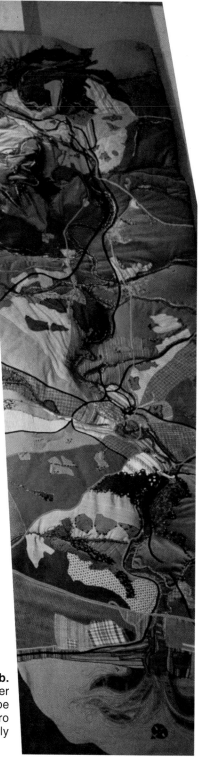

(110) 4 November 1977: Brunswick Square This former Unitarian burial ground has been cleared to make an open space, probably in connection with flats behind the camera. Unfortunately budget cuts have prevented its proper maintenance. The best pennant ledgers are submerged and Latimer's headstone is engulfed, the direction sign removed [**3/108, 12/101**].

(111) Summer 1977: St James's Churchyard, long cleared, another green lung with Farmer & Dark's National Farmers Union offices. 1 of only 6 of the 250 post-war office blocks which did not involve unacceptable demolitions and was distinguished; this one became an essential part of the conservation area. It was demolished in '95 for a larger block, making a nonsense of the conservation area.

(112) 11.25am 23 August 1977: Dowry Square This residents' open space in contrast only has to face traffic pollution! View of the centrepiece is now obscured [**8/25**].

(113) 2.50pm 7 October 1977: The Portway under the Suspension Bridge, before the erection of the tunnel canopy. Objections were made against Avon County for not consulting on such an intrusive proposal.

(114) 1977: Hanham Methodist Chapel Perhaps the most ignominious act by a congregation in the period was the demolition of this Georgian chapel and its horrific replacement.

(115) June 1977: St Monica's Home of Rest, Westbury Rd Sir Geo. Oatley's Elizabethan exercise, a typical omission of the 1977 Statutory List. Fortunately later spot-listed.

(116) Nov. 1977: Whiteladies Road Trinity Methodist Chapel demolished for Meryl Court flats. The belfry stage became a conservation area *memento mori*, (see below).

(117) 12.00am 6 April 1980: Whiteladies Road Poorly designed Meryl Court. Can the Methodists, with their newly won ecclesiastical exemption, be relied upon?

(118) April 1977: Baldwin Street, St Nicholas' Church The reuse of this church was an early success as a branch of Bristol Museums. After a funding crisis it runs as a Tourist Information Centre. Shrapnel damage is preserved on the cleaned south wall, but the Angel fountain still awaits reinstatement [40/45]. This fine shot was taken before the modern and most cluttered traffic light installation in the City marred this end of Bristol Bridge [39/198].

(119) May 1977: Blackboy Hill
Former school, then Avon Social Services, had its roof tiles replaced to match thanks to Avon's conservation officer. The K6 'phone box dem. but the 1904 fountain is listed.

(120) 1977: Queen's Parade, Brandon Hill Another school, still in use, in need of sympathetic control. The site, right, most crudely infilled.

(121) May 1977: Mark Lane
A more unusual view of the Lord Mayor's Chapel. The case for the churches in the hands of the City to be regularly repaired has been made.

(122) & (123) above & below - Broad Quay The Bristol & West two blocks had consent in the '60's when road widening came before conservation. Hope of saving Gabriel's Garrick's Head was therefore nil.

(124) 11.20am 10 January 1977: Park Street A gas explosion did for Nos 2, 4 & 6 Park Street, dating from the viaduct over Frog Lane. Now rebuilt in replica, except No. 6 which remains an empty site.

(125) August 1977: St George's Road Great Western Hotel, by RS Pope, 1837. Roman *civitas* always hidden in a bowl [27/76]. Seen before facading.

(126) below - August 1977: St George's Road Bristol Royal Workshops for the Blind. A remarkable group in a conservation area, demolished in 1993 one suspects to prevent spot-listing and without a signed contract for development. Another example of wilful damage to conservation areas. The Blind Asylum workshops on Hill Street of *c*.1912 were reduced in 1936 in order to extend St George's Rd to Park St and refronted with this fine design.

(127), (128) above & below May 1977: Kingsdown Above the high rise promised as a result of the clearances [**38/p38**]. This left precious survivals, such as Prospect House below, which became a case in the 1980's.

Alfred Place Kingsdown In the '80's the author often sketched too. The fact this Georgian lamp bracket at No. 6 (see right) was not saved was symptomatic of the case.

(129) 12.15pm 28 February 1977: Alfred Place, Kingsdown The end of a late C18 listed terrace, Nos 6 & 8, blitzed left and right. Infill had been proposed, but the scheme turned into dem. on dubious grounds of safety.

(130) 1977: Marlborough Hill, Kingsdown In the 70's this was not an unusual occurrence - not commercial salvage, but house owners rescuing Georgian fabric from the demolition ball - ordered by the Area Health Authority.

(131) right - 1977: Lower Ashley Road Spillers French factory before demolition.

(132) 1977: Ashley Grove Road, Baptist Mills Bleak new housing opposite Brooks cleaners, now more enclosed.

(133) November 1977: Brunswick Square, the austere east side of 1786, from the Neo-Classical entrance, now most unsatisfactorily closed up, to the former Unitarian burial ground (**110**). The dominant and very Bristol Georgian architecture of brick, above setts and pennant paving.

(134) 29 May 1977: King Street and its famous townscape of discrete styles from the most compromising angle! No. 35, brick warehouse, left, has been newly refurbished as offices. St Nicholas' Almshouses, centre, will be vacated in 1993 and Coopers' Hall set to receive new vases early in 1996.

(135) June 1977: St Paul Street looking at the return elevation of the end block on the south side of Portland Square. The Square is Bathstone, St Paul Street brick and Wilson Street 'Bristol Black' roughcast -the 3 local C18 materials. This latter finish is now rare; witness the 1995 public inquiry into the proposed demolition of the fine house on the left and the rest of the terrace which had been deliberately left to rot.

(136) & (137) above & left July 1977: Corn Street
One of the worst pieces of customer relations was National Westminster Bank's facading and rebuilding of listed No. 36 Corn Street, by Gingell, 1864. Why was listed building consent granted?

(138) & (139) top right & right 4 March 1977: Old Market Street
No. 46, Raselle, pawnbrokers, and below the listed row of three shops with their good shopfronts at the Midland Road junction.
Refurbishment at first appeared to threaten closure of the pawnbrokers, but they reopened in Stapleton Road. Refurbishment ruined the backs of this row and created a too assertive building on the corner site.

(140) July 1977: **Park Street** The viaduct is being repainted and the Royal Hotel and Trinity Street await redevelopment.

(144) & (145) above & below - 4.05pm 14 September 1977 & May 1977: **The Grove** Brewers have not treated historic pubs kindly. Only the look-out of the Hole-in-the-Wall remains of interest [**8/99**]. **The Bunch of Grapes, Denmark St** lost its etched glass without consent.

(141) 1977: **Temple Meads** Former Bristol & Exeter Railway offices, SC Fripp 1852 [**9/68**] before refurb. in the '80's, to be followed by PVCu windows.

(142) May 1977: **Lower College Street** looking to Queen's Parade and Washington House. Leaded 4-star petrol 81.5p/gallon!

(143) May 1977: **Priory Rd, Shirehampton** Imitation stone cladding on brick and terracotta, before parked cars and wheelie bins.

(146) August 1977: Canon's Road The Dome in the car park of the tobacco bonds. It was designed and built for fibreglass yacht construction for £2,000 (**269**) and sold on for reuse after a year. It was inflated to 0.5psi by 2x60 watt fans. Probably the first instance of post-commercial docks architecture and, leaving a clean site, one of the best.

(147) 1977: Canon's Road U & V Sheds; future home of the Exhibition Centre. Conservation area application for dem. is pending!

(148) below right - November 1977: Merchants Road The Hydraulic Engine House to operate the North Junction Lock, *c.*1870, by William Armstrong & Co. Schemes for reuse were invited and the resultant PH proved unexceptional.

(149) bottom right - 5.15pm 25 September 1977: Mardyke from Baltic Wharf Sailing school supersedes the traditional location for sea cadets.

(150) 1977: Winterbourne Lane Former Hambrook Brick Works, now demolished.

1978

(151) 1978: **Blaise Castle** The splendid Beech Grove, perhaps suffering the effects of the previous dry year.

Conservation Issues
Edgecumbe Hall, Queen's Road: 3rd inquiry
Host Street/Christmas Steps, C15/C17
  house, now chippy

New building in progress
Trinity Road police station
Park Street: Nos 2 & 4 rebuilt
Stoke Bishop: elderly persons' flats near
  Jubilee fountain
Eastfield Road: new houses on playing field
  site
Knowle: Methodist church hall
Ham Green: 100 pottery kilns excavated

January
Kings Weston Lane: Rothwell House dem.
Whiteladies Road: Trinity Methodist church
  demolished
A38/Gypsy Patch Lane: flyover opened
La Retraite school fire
Grit bins arrive, four months late
Hotwells: Stoke House, scheme for offices
  and 24 flats to rear
Redland Hill: Queen Victoria Maternity
  Hospital to become offices on appeal, at
  first for Regional Hospital Board. Raises
  fears for more offices in residential conser-
  vation areas

February
Filton: subway opened from BAC to post
  office
Portway and Bridge Valley Road closed
Wells Road/West Town Lane roadworks
Worst blizzards in west country for 30 years

March
High Street: plaque unveiled to indicate site
  of High Cross
Gaol Ferry slip: 5-ton yacht launched
Ashley Hill: Witts (Salvation Army/Blue
  Maids) demolished
Whitchurch: Asda supermarket opened
Bishopsworth: Rowe's builders' merchants,
  converted to Leo's supermarket
Prince's Wharf: M shed converted to
  Industrial Museum opened for City's
  technology collections
Broad Quay: Sedan Chair PH reopened by
  RW after refurbishment

St Paul Street: Nos 15-21 to be demolished & replaced in replica

Avon Gorge Hotel, Clifton: additional bedrooms and car parking

City Docks: Hotwell Dock housing redevelopment

Alfred Place/Portland Street: scheme for 6 flats

Montpelier Conservation Area proposed

Queen's Road: Beacon House (formerly JF Taylor's) facadism for Habitat after demolition application refused

Stoke Cliffe House, Stapleton: CAP prefers no further development in Frome Valley

Host Street warehouse: CAP regrets loss of end bay of warehouse, subsequently given consent

City Museum & Art Gallery: proposal to replace Edwardian entrance doors thwarted by RW

April

Royal Portbury Dock: year's strike ends

College Green: new traffic control

Captain Webb memorial glass from Portland Chapel reset in Lutton Hall [**12/cover**]

King Square: Removal of decorative fanlight to No. 12 without consent, now proposed as offices

City Docks: Opportunities report supported by CAP and calls for conservation area designation [**38/337**] are repeated in order to 'control the demolition of many fine unlisted buildings...'

Cyclebag - Channel your calf & leg energies Bristol Action Group: cycleroute provision, the opening of parks & footways to cyclists

First regular radio broadcasts of Parliament

WHO declares world free of smallpox. English woman dies in September from virus leaked from smallpox laboratory.

May

Vaulted Chambers, Castle Park, opened on May Day only

Cribbs Causeway, Carrefour hypermarket (later Asda) opened

Postmen vote to resist Sunday collections

June

SS *Great Britain* receives one-millionth visitor

Council surrenders half-share in bus company

Clarence Road, St Philip's: dual carriageway

Prince Street: The Shakespeare PH refurbished

City Docks: Baltic Wharf Leisure Centre opened

Pill to Keynsham river walkway opened

Jubilee celebrations of Coronation include planting of Old Vic courtyard, Avon Walkway (a *20 Idea*), reopening of some rooms of Ashton Court

World Environment Day, 5th

July

City Docks: floating restaurants opened in MV *Lochiel*, Canon's Marsh and LV 89 (the Lightship), Welsh Back

Brislington Vicarage: over-intensive housing development

Old Market: refurbishment of north side dependent for funding on outstanding conservation area status

Trim Trail erected on the Downs and the wych elms endangered by Dutch elm disease

St Michael's Hill: University gap sites decried again (still gapped in 1995)

Avonmouth & Severnside: 5-year pollution study announced by Public Protection Committee

Lib-Lab pact ends

World's first test-tube baby born in Oldham

Devolution Bills for Scotland and Wales receive royal assent

August

Rubbish crisis; all tips full

Guinea Street: Ostrich PH refurbished and extended to left, resulting in loss of an infamous cider pub with bus seats and sawdust for locals, sailors and students

Warwick Road, Warwick Arms PH: Avon seeks demolition consent of listed building

St Philip & St Jacob extension proposed, masking important south side of church

September

Victorian Society Avon Group formed

Portway: Civic Society calls for rock scaling and any protective structures to be subject to planning permission. Also suggested that River Avon is used for refuse transfer, rather than by lorry through residential areas

City Docks: Courage gain waterside tables at Ostrich PH, docks get clutter

Hippodrome: Moss Empire reopens, temporarily

Temple Meads Old Station joint working party

Worrall Road: St John's school opened

Whiteladies Rd: Whiteladies cinema reopens with three screens

Wells Road: Harris & Tozer to close

Castle Park plaque unveiled

October

Horsefair/Merchant Street: Peter Robinson/Etam becomes Orlando

Newfoundland Road demolitions for dual carriageway

November

Broad Quay: Garrick's Head PH demolished for Bristol & West extension

Windmill Hill City Farm stocked with 50 animals & warden/farmer

Lewin's Mead Unitarian Chapel: Civic Society publishes statement of this great rationalist work of a

prison architect, W Blackburn; new uses still sought

Lower Union Street: Broadmead Chapel spire of 1957 taken down

78-100 St Michael's Hill: Health Authority's listed rotting row restored only after direct action campaigner prosecuted for painting up woodwork

Manor House, Park Lane, St Michael's, listed, burnt shortly after a closing order imposed leads to suspicions

60-65 Redcliff Street (formerly Edwards, Ringer & Biggs) converted to small business use (listed, suffered fire, in 1993)

Temple Meads Old Station advertised To Let

Portland Square: Nos 7 & 8 to be facaded

General Synod votes down ordination of women

December

Queen's Road: The Berkeley reopens as Reception Suite. Subsequently receives cast-iron canopy without conservation area consent, removed 1994

Queen's Road: Maggs suffers IRA bombing (also Coventry, Manchester, Southampton)

Fairfax Street: another bomb safely detonated

Passage Road, W-O-T: milestone recut

Falcondale Road/Greystoke Ave: removal of bottleneck involves loss of slag-topped wall.

(152) March 1978: Brandon Steps Working gas lantern on its original bracket

(153) March 1978: Lodge Street looking east to the front elevation of C17 10 Lower Park Row, its windows blocked. The house, right, on Lodge St and school beyond were sacrificed for access as part of the Lodge St scheme.

(154) 1978: St Augustine's Place The Georgianised rears of the C15/16 timber-framed houses that were part of the Tramways offices, before facading and redevelopment. These were finished in 'Bristol Black' roughcast.

(155) February 1978: Dighton Street
The finest house east of Lunsford House, Park Row (**189**) was Harford's Palladian town house of *c*.1760. Later an RC convent, with prominent chapel reduced to a capped wall, left [**18/131**]. By '78 it was overdeveloped and styled Montague Court as co-ownership flats. Note the fine Georgian forecourt walls, to which no care was given or required to be given as a condition of consent.

(156) 1978: King Square
Ill-used ever since the Kingsdown clearances and now redeveloped to the left, with a less than discreet piece of 'fitting-in'. Requiring good manners as a planning condition is proving very difficult in the Bristol of the '90's, not least for the Georgian Group. The Square has been much improved by the recent reinstatement of the railings.

(157) March 1978: Cumberland Street, north side. Great efforts were made, successfully, to condemn these buildings, quite unjustifiably. Any C18 building which is unscaffolded (only 2 are tied here at 2nd floor) is capable of <u>repair</u>. It was pitiful that the professionals responsible had no interest in them as listed buildings. As a result this, and other terraces were lost and rebuilt as fakery.

(158) March 1978: Gloucester Street leading south out of Brunswick Square. This row of late C18 houses with the usual Bristol emphasis of red brick fronts and Bristol Black 'book ends' to the side elevations, and the adjacent photograph **(161)** was what was referred to as the 'ring of dereliction', which the Joint Conservation Programme would tackle. These houses received a steel frame in the centre pair in conversion to offices - a ridiculous solution guaranteed to interfere with the interiors - and this photograph was used by the author to have the arched glazing bars reinstated which, by the '80's, had disapppeared.

(159) below - 1978: Brook Road looking into Montpelier. As with Kingsdown the hillside provides a backdrop, here of smaller scale and more intact. Derelict Lower Cheltenham Place, centre, beyond the neat mid C19 terraces of Brook Road, with the view stopped by a 3-storey centrepiece, all make for good townscape.

(160) right - September 1978: Pritchard Street, west side, here being made safe. A terrace with an Edwardian centrepiece (an interesting development of the historic street) and not only ironed out in rebuilding - everything else Georgian, both west and east sides, was demolished and rebuilt in inaccurate replica on steel frames in the '80's.

(161) March 1978: Brunswick Square south side, fine brick-work with Gibbs surrounds to the book-ends (here no longer black) of 1766 by E Workman, with the derelict side of Gloucester Street **(157)** off to the left. This too was subjected to developers' interests: Demolition refused at public inquiry; later granted save for 2 frontages; after rebuilding the garden side to Bond St was redeveloped 'back to back', achieving 2 sites in 1!

(162) below, centre - March 1978: Jamaica Street Dereliction of listed buildings on a smaller scale, later ironed out by a housing association. Here, as generally, the housing association movement never addressed conservation.

(163) March 1978: Jacob's Wells Road In the process of moving to (or from?) a listed Georgian house... The site of Bristol's first theatre was mooted to be in the premises of the Bristol Carpet Cleaning Co., but this seems unlikely, according to those who have made a search. The carpet cleaners closed down not long after this shot was taken.

(164) March 1978: Picton Street, Montpelier Picton Lodge, due to be converted to flats, dates from the Regency before Picton Street was built, confining the Lodge.

(165) right - October 1978: Picton Lodge, seen between the Charley Box, left [**12/35**], and the 'Bristol Black' roughcast bookend of the street terrace.

(166) June 1978: Park Place, Clifton A coach-house to the rear of Richmond Terrace. As a so-called 'curtilege building', it was only protected by planning and conservation area controls. Note the scale in relation to the Gothick doorway.

(167) October 1980: Park Place, Clifton The denouement to (**166**). The principle of conversion to a dwelling apart, the slate roof, gable and surround of the Gothick doorway have been demolished, rebuilt and enlarged with a tile roof. The result is typically ugly and certainly not Clifton.

(168) March 1978: Mornington Rd to Anglesea Place Setts, 'Bristol Black' distant, & quietude

(169) March 1978: Alfred Hill An endstop then of black dash, now also bereft of its wood sashes!

(170) November 1978: St George's Rd A listed pair dem. without consent. The author later recovered Peters, builders, Brilliant fascia.

(171) March 1978: Jacob's Wells Road The pair of houses, bottom right, were demolished for a school theatre.

(172) August 1978: St Paul's Church Declared redundant in the previous year and in '95 still not with an acceptable new use, although schemes for a design studio were mooted. Bevan's gothic revival east window sits incongruously in the chancel of this yet Gothick interior, despite removal of its side galleries and high pews. What a focus this must have been to residents of the once elegant Square.

(173) March 1978: St James' Conservation Area, most put upon enclave in the '90's with new offices. NFU offices (111) peep behind the church, the tower possibly refaced with stone from Bristol Castle. EH tried to stop the unsatisfactory work in the church in the '90's. Ralph Edward's Eye Hospital, left, was to be replaced with something bigger but of lesser merit.

(174) March 1978: Brunswick Square Former Brunswick Square Congregational Chapel by William Armstrong, 1834, occupies the whole of one side of the Square. It was a Christian Science church before conversion and flooring-in for offices. The manse, left, also converted.

(175) February 1978: Filton Road Former Horfield Barracks chapel, 1847, by Butterfield. Converted to offices & further developed on appeal.

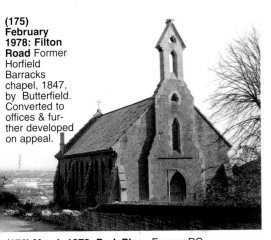

(176) March 1978: Park Place Former RC Bishop's palace, derelict ever since.

(177) 25 November 1978: Tailors' Court - Tailors' Hall, 1740, right. When is this guildhall going to have its inserted floor removed? **(280)**

(178) July 1978: Small Street The General Post Office, WJ Williams of London, 1868, his only known work in the city, before dem. and facading for the Law Courts against advice [**38/p15**]. Especially good cut lettering over the entry, not reinstated.

(179) 25 November 1978: St George's Road The C19 profile of Pope's Royal Western Hotel in association with Brunel, before facading, with the characteristic hillside ever present beyond [**18/253**]. The 'temporary' car parks linger on awaiting a climate for further massive speculative office development on land acquired post-war by compulsory purchase.

(180) left - March 1978: Jacob's Wells Road Foster & Wood's institutional Tudor QEH of 1843, before cast-iron windows were replaced with PVCu. The vital enclosure of the great stone retaining wall was reduced by the transparent design of the new theatre (off left).

(181) March 1978: Rosebery Terrace QEH extension in pale machine-made bricks runs in right, set above the rubblestone of the raised pavement and below Foster & Wood's school building.

(182) March 1978: Richmond Dale, Clifton The Mission House & Reading Room, *c.*1870, perhaps then also a school - a good example of the genre and unlisted. Does a reader know its history? At the time in new ownership and the garden being cleared.

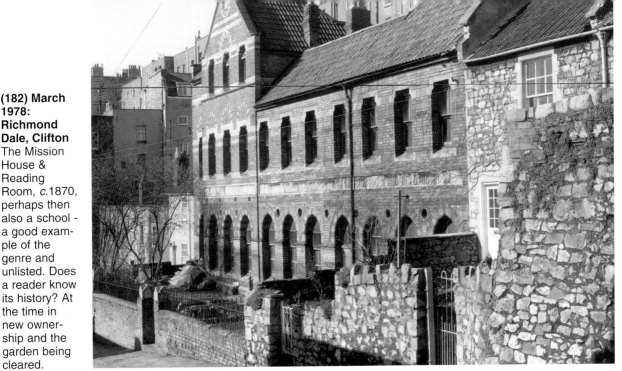

(183) March 1978: Park Row The former Coliseum Picture House of 1912 clings on; its skating rink neighbour of 1910 dem. Cleaned with grant in 1993, will the 1995 facading reinstate the stone balustraded parapet?

(184) March 1978: White-ladies Road from formerly disreputable Woodbury Lane. SR Selman, butchers at No.150 opposite, removed their famous *By Appointment* in Brilliant lettering [**12/146**] (Victoria's 1896 order for Osborne) for this aluminium shopfront. Not long afterwards the business closed. Another genuine C19 painted sign is just visible high on the side wall: R Thinson, gents' cycle maker.

(185) December 1978: Redland Road Strachan's unaltered gateway to Redland Court of 1735 with its stone icicles and fine wrought gates, grade II*, closing the vista through Lover's Walk to a castellated arch. Possible arch fragments are in a garden building of Archfield Court.

(186) April 1978: St Nicholas' Market These stalls may date from 1745, with zinc canopies perhaps pre-dating the glass roof of 1855 (**194**). Unfortunately much of this Georgian joinery was replaced in replica in the '80's.

(187) March 1978: Westerleigh area A model pennant stone barn of *c.*1800 with half-hip roof, now dem. In 1980 SPAB mounted a national campaign to save historic barns and keep them in working use. The author was a survey organiser for Avon.

He appeared at 3 public inquiries against planning authorities and owners seeking des. res. consents. Englishcombe tithe barn was saved; at Almondsbury the scheme reduced; at Marshfield Sec. of State Ridley thought he knew better than his Inspector.

(189) April 1978: Park Row
Glorious Lunsford House, *c.*1725 and later, remained hidden from the author until 1978. Alone surviving of those great early Georgian houses to overlook the city [**11/9**], it dearly needs expert care, and some decent planting!

(190) April 1978: King Street Nos 7 & 8, offices of Moxley, Jenner & Ptrs., authors of the facelift scheme for the Tramways offices (**21**), here doing likewise. Presently the offices of EH.

(188) left & (191) right - July 1978: West Mall
This was the first of 5 years of the Clifton Fayre, in aid of reinstatement of the railings to the central gardens, seen on the table to the left. The Fayre became so successful that, coinciding as it did with the Wine Fair and thus competing with it, the City applied street vendor licence requirements. The railings were completed but it was decided not to continue with the Fayre.

(192) 6.05pm 5 June 1978: Christmas Street, St Bartholomew's Hospital Roger Price, Bristol Museums archaeologist, explains the standing south-east arcade of a hall (view of inner face), with its Romanesque columns and capitals to the B&GAS, and the late Robert Knapp, Bristol Hon. Sec., digests it. The dating of this early hall remains problematic. A grant-aided scheme, much was carefully preserved in redevelopment.

(193) 1978: St Bartholomew's Gateway The Early English Madonna and Child before removal to the inside of the porch for safety. The owners of the site, a group of local charities, are believed to have tried to sell the listed sculpture, but the gaff was swiftly blown!

(194) April 1978: St Nicholas' Market after hours. Facelift-coloured stalls and fine glazed roof by RS Pope, 1855, abut a finer Corn Exchange [**40/cover**].

(195) April 1978: Victoria Street No. 16 hangs on 5 years after an inquiry decision [**38/381**]. Nos 18-22, right, wrongly condemned, are still upright!

(196) 1978: Orchard Lane warehouses from behind Pipe Lane. Fine pennant rubblestone warehouses, *c.* 1825, in the ownership of Bristol Municipal Charities. This 2nd phase of St Augustine's redevelopment equally ruined these unlisted buildings. The scheme was described by the consultant as 'retention' - of what one may ask? The author acquired an 18ft door to the former gateway [**2/114**]; a dated lead rainhead was neither for sale nor reinstated. The result is a conservation parody.

(197) April 1978: Kingsdown Pde. Nos 65-81, formerly Nos 1-9 St James' Place 1797, a Patyian series of linked pairs, with triple centrepiece, now mostly stuccoed and on the up.

(200) below - 1979: Manor House, St Michael's, early C18, gutted by fire in '79. One of the few grant jobs properly repaired, by Architecton and John Schofield.

(199) April 1978: Canon's Road A buy-out of Imperial by a group with interests in Lloyds Bank, turned this into an unexpected and unwanted office site in the conservation area. The tobacco bonds were dem. and offices built around an incongruous arena, a la *20 Ideas*.

(198) *c*.1978: Whitehouse Lane On the down - late C19 dignified housing in tuck-pointed brick. Demolished for industrial units.

(202) below - October 1978: Old Market Open-fronted wholesale butchers before closure, forced by exposure to traffic pollution? Now a shop. C17 Masons Arms PH, right.

(201) 11.00am 10 August 1977: Cumberland Rd Seward's 1832 Gaol gatehouse; curtain walls survive to the east.

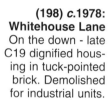

(203) left - May 1978: Kings Weston Lane Wintour House maisonettes shortly before first refit. These blocks came to their useful end in the early '90's.

(204) above - September 1978: Station Road, Henbury In contrast these earlier medium rise local authority flats, Henbury Court, were much more successful, being well modelled and set in the remains of old parkland. Henbury Stables extreme left.

(205) 1978: Kings Weston Road Rockwell House from the rear garden, during demolition. This unlisted 1870's house had been the University of Bath School of Management Studies who sold it to a house builder. **(206) September 1978: Rockwell Ave.** The new speculative housing by Architecton for the house builder, innovative and refreshingly free of present-day house builders' mono-culture houses, universally applied.

(207) top, left - July 1978: Portway during safety work removing loose material from the face of the Gorge at Bridge Valley Road junction.

(208) above - July 1978: Hotwell Road enjoying the quietude of the extended road closure for rock clearing. Although some landing stages remain, the departure shed and the signalling mast went in the '80's.

(209) left - July 1978: Brunel Lock Road The dirtiest job in the Docks? - cleaning the 1884 Grid-iron in evening light. This is placed in the line of Jessop's 1804 lock. In the foreground is Brunel's lock of 1844.

(210) opposite - February 1978: Canon's Road Demolishing Glasgow or T Shed (the gable remains of another, fire-damaged shed, left). The MV *Lochiel* newly arrived.

(211) April 1978: Canon's Marsh
The GWR Goods Shed from under the steel canopy looking at the ferro-cement terminus and warehouse by Mouchel-Hennebique, 1904-6, showing the platforms, now removed. Conservationists have rightly resisted attempts to demolish this building listed in 1992 for its pioneering reinforced concrete system, in connection with 'Harbourside' redevelopment.

(212) July 1977: Canon's Marsh An ex-Italian (?) army ambulance, YWB 494M, in front of the in-situ concrete GWR Goods Shed and offices, right.

(213) opposite - November 1978: Sand Wharf, Hotwells Breaking-up the grab and hoppers.

(214) November 1978: Redcliff Backs WCA
Warehouse by WA Brown, 1909-13, grade II.
Another early use of reinforced concrete, particularly for the lucams (seen here with the
landing platform in place below). Long derelict,
it was the subject of a unsatisfactory design
competition (no exhibition of schemes) in 1983,
and grants were not taken up nor work commenced until 1995.

**(215) February 1978:
Hotwells** A working
steam tug, SS *Goliath*
- something of a rarity -
arrives towing in
LV89. Here she is
seen leaving the City
Dock having delivered
her charge. The red
painted Lightship
became a public
house on Welsh Back,
until, no longer viable
and no longer an his-
toric vessel (by virtue
of conversion), she
was towed to the
breakers in May 1995.

(216) March 1978: Perry Road
A green Bristol model L5G chassis with Easton Coachworks (Lowestoft) body, LHY 976, of December 1949 date, leads a Rag procession. Note the City coat of arms on the bodywork, dispensed with in 1963.

(217) March 1978: Perry Road
Four Rag procession floats pass the Red Lodge, perhaps more lorry than float than in previous years. The Red Lodge used of course to be roughcast-plastered and colourwashed red. Vestiges of the red ochre on the walls can be found on close inspection. Perhaps one day the aesthetic and physical merits of replastering will be realised once again.

(218) June 1979: Stourhead The C15 High Cross, erected here in 1765.

Conservation Issues

Wells Road: farmhouse adjacent Little Thatch
Armoury Square: Georgian houses
Prince Street: Merchants' houses
Blackboy Hill, St Vincent's Hill: cottages

1 Freeland Place, Hotwells
Medieval Cross, 1764, re-erected at Stourhead, taken down by NT against advice of SPAB for fears of over-restoration and loss of ancient colour
Listed buildings in Avon increased 889 in last two years, to total of 10,590, the highest density outside Greater London (July)

New building in progress

Broad Quay House, CWS site and Bristol & West Building Society extension opposite
Cheltenham Road: Colston's Girls' School extension,
Lower Castle Street: Frome House
Suspension Bridge: Gallery over A4
Merchants Road, Hotwells: housing
West Town Lane: housing
Whiteladies Gate shopping centre
Feeder Road, Midland Road and York Road: industrial units
Garden exhibition at V & A

January

Upper Maudlin St: Welsh Baptist Chapel demolished
Unity Street reopened (closed since explosion December 1977)
York Road/St Luke's Road: east corner widened
York Road/Bath Bridge: factory demolished
E Shed, St Augustine's Reach, restored. Poorly laid walkway setts removed 1994
Jacob Street Brewery: CAP asks for restoration if adjacent office development is permitted. Permitted but not restored
Bishop's Knoll site: development proposed

City Docks: competition for 200 houses on Baltic Wharf announced; 83 schemes submitted later in the year. Winner not built
Avon County opposes office reconstructions in Portland Square Conservation Area preferring industrial uses between Orange Street and Newfoundland Street
CPAB reports Planning Officer asked to take up instances of painted stonework in CA's
CAP discusses the plight of pennant paving, a subject which rolls on and on until an untenable proposal is adopted 10 years later of city-wide removal and redistribution, against all known conservation ethics

February

Trinity Road police station opened by Princess Alexandra. Following month 1869 memorial tablet to murdered policeman from Holy Trinity Church set up in station **[16/104]**
Temple Meads Old Station:Inaugural meeting of Brunel Engineering Heritage Trust. British Railways appoint architect to do feasibility study
Old Market, Council and Bristol Municipal Charities, as major land owners on north side, commission study proposing small scale commercial use in rehabilitated (actually facaded) historic frontages and residential development on backland
Severn House, Hallen: demolition by developer, who had bought knowing refurb. to be a condition of development, opposed
Hotwell Road: Trinity Rooms housing development proposed
Bristol: an architectural history by Gomme, Jenner & Little published, commenced 1968, with some illustrations by RW. The first comprehensive study of Bristol architecture

March

Berkeley Cafe tea dances resumed

2 & 4 Park Street reopen

Callington Road (West Town Lane by-pass) opens

Sheene Road: Simmette's soap factory demolished

Queen's Road: Dingles refurbishment starts

CAP asks P&TCommittee to remind City Eng. that statutory undertakers and his own dept are made aware of the delineation of Conservation Areas to prompt reinstatement of paving, Bristol being one of the top ten towns with historic environment.

Street Lighting Superintendent advises CAP that it was not intended to replace existing gas lamps at this stage but it had been necessary where gas mains were corroded

Avon Conservation of Resources Network set up by FoE and the Conservation Society

Three Mile Island radiation leak

April

Portway reopens

The Metropole resumes as cinema with ethnic following

Suspension Bridge: bungy jump by local members of Dangerous Sports Club

Whiteladies Road: CAP recommends BBC appoint an architect for their redevelopment

10 Lower Park Row: demolition application of grade II house of 'Tudor origins' halted by author's objection

Conservation Programme: HBC offers increase of £236,000 in grant aid

May

Greystoke Avenue: houses replace prefabs

Newfoundland Road widened for M32 extension

Westleaze, Long Ashton: parish

council attempts to save mill

Bristol & Exeter Railway Co. offices cleared

Temple Meads Old Station, Brunel Heritage Centre collapses. Demolition for road widening refused

Prince's Wharf: Author's scheme for reuse of Cranes 29-32 for City Docks Ventures

Labour loses general election, Margaret Thatcher PM

June

Blackboy Hill garage rebuilt as filling station

Hope Chapel reopens as community centre

Kings Weston: **Echo** being repaired

Broad Plain: 2nd application, taking care of Nos 1-5 and 9 and instituting authorised vandalism of historic row

Avon CC tries to reduce extent of Old Market Conservation Area

Bradley House, Shirehampton: damaging conversion of stable block to form house

City Docks Conservation Area designated

Queen's Road, Edgecumbe Hall: Christian Scientists give up and sell - to be refurbished

July

2nd World Wine Festival and Clifton Fayre

St Augustine's Place: two listed BTCC properties demolished apparently without consent on corner of Pipe Lane in anticipation of redevelopment

Midland Road: 4.5 acres of setted surface off Midland Road ripped up in redevelopment, and much traditional hard landscaping fronting Midland Road goes too in due course in front of new industrial units

Urban Centre of Alternative Technology formed in Bedminster, for energy conservation & intensive food production

Civic Society makes RW its first Hon. life member

30's Society formed, later renamed The Twentieth Century Society

August

Camera Obscura reopens

SS *Great Britain* Committee elects RW as Hon. member

September

Street lighting: Avon 'upgrading' lighting in conservation areas with standard plastic cones, only mitigated by City Council paying the extra cost of repro. lanterns in streets of 'major importance'

Northavon vernacular house survey, pre-1720 by Linda Hall - progress report published; monograph publ. 1983. Good early study of newly categorised building type, but fails to result in proper conservation of any of the genre to date

October

Christmas Steps Nos 1, 1a & warehouse in Host Street restored & reduced respectively by Bristol Municipal Charities at £150K after their own neglect. 1st scheme of Joint Conservation Programme

Bishop's House (formerly Sir Geo. Oatley's house), Clifton Green: 'unsafe' vases removed from roof apparently without consent

Welsh Back: demolition of X shed for squash courts proposed

Pembroke Road, Clifton: conversion of All Saints' parish hall to flats proposed

Avon Gorge: County constructs gallery without planning permission, frustrating any comment on the design

Christmas Steps: office development proposed to close off bottom from Rupert Street

St George's Road: redevelopment, including proposed demolition of 2 listed houses. Later demolished without consent.

Marlborough Hill: Hospital Board applies to demolish No. 17, grade II. Bought and refurbished by a local architect.

Anglesea Place: partial demolition of school proposed

Boyce's Buildings, Clifton: refurb. scheme

November

Mount of Olives Pentecostal leave Blackboy Hill for St Saviour's, Chandos Road

Robertson's Jam factory, Brislington, to close

US on full nuclear alert; computer error

December

St Michael's, **Manor House**: hostel scheme in gutted C17/18 house

Mounted police issued with new style helmet

George's bookshop erects a clock (a name to be lost in 1994)

Old Library in King Street opens as a restaurant

43-45 Queen Square: warehouses demolished for speculative offices prompting debate in Avon Conservation News

Gloucester Rd: Bailey's Stores close

Worrall Road: CAP opposes Avon CC's demolition of original St John's School (unlisted)

Prince Street: Prince's Hall demolition application refused

Tucker Street: covered shopping redevelopment proposed. Site progressively cleared of buildings, still undeveloped in '95

Avon Metro first mooted

Three Lamps Junction: Avon County designs £4.7m interchange; simplified in 1979

The Centre: King George V Memorial funds to be expended on a fountain and paving at the end of Narrow Quay

(219) April 1978: Acton Court, Iron Acton The most important house case in Avon which ran through the '80's. The story of its salvation will be covered in *BAIW 1981-85*. **(220) July 1979:** The farmer-owner in the C16 courtiers' entry. Courted by several conservation-architects, he kept the great pile propped up.

(221) & (223) August 1979, (222) June 1980: Over Court, Over
The C16 house was boarded up after the war, let go and demolished when a final rescue failed. 1 of 40 deer parks in Avon, the latter day deer park now looks more like a govt. plant, than a park.

(**223**) Below is the view from the former fishponds.

(224) March 1978: 10 Lower Park Row
The view from Perry Road of the Georganised front of a house of 'Tudor origins', when the demolition application was pending. As a case Bristol's equivalent of Acton Court, coming at the start of the Joint Conservation Programme

(225) & (226) January & December 197
10 Lower Park Row Left, a lower ground plain, 12-panel Jacobean door (the house dat from 1660's) subsequently stolen, like other d tive panelled doors, due to a failure to secure property after its importance was known. Walk into a hitherto unknown Jacobean interior (init as a trespasser and unequipped for photogra the centre of Bristol was humbling. Above, a f floor room after investigation; the stone windo mullions have been robbed. The door frame is fact C17 stopped and moulded.

(227) & (228) July 1979: St Augustine's Place Nos 2 & 3, C17 & C18, listed. Wrongly described as of 'little architectural importance' by the consultant and apparently demolished without consent in order to facilitate redevelopment.

(229) 1979: Trooper's Hill, Crew's Hole Bristol & West Tar Distillers' site, now filled with incongruous blocks of flats engineered by the BDC.

(230) January 1979: Anchor Road Rowe Bros' right, dem. for offices, 10 Bond left, dem. '95, for a development site against conservation area policy, with the permission of the City Council and in the face of objections.

(231) 6.15pm 18 May 1979: Gas Ferry Road The SS *Great Britain* fitted with her replica 6-blade propeller. Note the condition of the wooden rudder.

(232) June 1979: Wells Road Tony Benn opens the Totterdown Centre, a group of traders operating from a row of shops, newly refurbished by Keith Hallett.

(233) & (234) 10 December 1979: Old Market Street
These C17 timber-framed survivals had been let go by their owners (dem. was stopped in May 1972 by a demo.) and it was thanks to the HBC that they were the first buildings identified as able to be saved through a Joint Conservation Programme. In the event the vestigial timber frames were not repaired and were sacrificed, as was John Goss's shopfront at Nos 38 &39 [**38/248**]. Note the shutters, now gone, at No.42 [**5/112, 18/77**].

(237) January 1979: Gloucester Rd, Avonmouth The lesser, but fine, Royal Hotel.

(236) 5.45pm 24 June 1979: Ashton Court 1929 8-litre Hispano Suiza, one of Reece's favourite cars on show.

(235) February 1979: Beckspool Road
Clarendon House, the garden recently cleared, prior to conversion to a nursing home.

(238) July 1979: College Green The storm clouds gather over the Royal Hotel. Redevelopment was first mooted of WA Hawtin's 1865 hotel. A planning brief was prepared which resulted in a 'cross-subsidised' hotel and office development. But this produced a hotel extension of mediocre materials, artificial stone and PVCu windows. Bristol lost industrial Anchor Road and a church site.

(239) 1978: Stokes Croft Work did not start on this listed row Nos 59-69 until 1979, when No. 59 was refurbished, but removing the footway alongside and losing decorative plaster cornices.

(240) 1979: Bedminster Down Arup Associates HQ for CEGB, 1 of 2 major new HQ buildings. CEGB was a forerunner in heat recovery design.

(241) February 1979: Arno's Court Reeve's Black Castle, made of black slag, seen after grant-aided refurb. to a PH. Note the inappropriate door colour. Became an infamous BDC case in '95.

(242) April 1979: Lower Church Lane, St Michael's The former rectory, grade II, Gothick refronting by Paty in haired ash plaster, before sale and grant-aided refurb. Little Gothick flourishes over the cornice were carelessly cut away and the elevation cemented.

(243) & (244) October 1980: The former rectory kitchen block in 'Bristol Black', possibly C17, with arguably the earliest surviving spit rack in the central area (right). Does this survive? [**4/111**].

(246) 1979: Wade Street, looking north-west to Newfoundland Street. Tollgate House looms again over the remains of Bristol's first planned suburb, 1700-20 - 4 streets: Great & Little Anne Street, bisected by Wade Street.

(245) 10 December 1979: Wellington Road Tollgate House, 1975 (Bristol's biggest office block until the fractionally larger Castlemead), looms over this course of the culverted Frome.

(247) July 1980: Wade Street No.17, 1700-20, with C19 shopfront. Along with the Swan with Two Necks PH, the only survivors from this early suburb (**246**), left, and unlisted.

(248) *c.*1976: **Trinity Road** The Hannah More School with the 1866 police station beyond, the second in St Philip's, eventually both demolished for the new station.

(249) *c.*1979: **Trinity Road** The first new police station, left, to be built by Avon & Somerset Constabulary, opened 1 February 1979 by Princess Alexandra - a very different conception to Holy Trinity by T Rickman, 1829-32.

(250) July 1979: Portwall Lane/Canynge Street corner No. 2 was interesting for its good example of tuck pointing, also present on Georgian Lunsford House (**189**), buildings in Portland Square etc. It effected first-class brickwork from seconds (see below). Conservation of such pointing is rare. These seemly buildings were demolished for an inept car showroom.

(251) July 1979: Canynge Street Tuck pointing on No.2. Pure lime putty was applied, ruled and plumbed into irregular joints, or actually over the brick face.

(252) February 1979: Bath Road, looking to Mardons' factories at the start of demolition. Foreground left is the link line to St Philip's Marsh railyard. Mardons rebuilt on the same site after most of their factories on the site were targeted in 1940 (they were known to be printers of Ordnance maps and high on the Luftwaffe list). The site was eventually redeveloped as a housing scheme. The Mead Street GWR sheds, left, were demolished in 1980.

(253) & (254) July 1979: Hempton Lane, Almondsbury

Henry Williams' work of 1897 in Clare Street had been reclaimed and adapted to form a house, Hempton Gables [**16/200**], which now found itself in the way of the burgeoning AZtec West business park, east of M5.

These were taken when boarded up, prior to demolition.

(255) October 1979: British Road, Bedminster One of those seemly, simple terraces (this one 1837) hanging on in Bedminster, end-stopped here to a front on British Road, Victoria Cottage. The late C19 traditional shopfront, T J Hewitt, greengrocers, has been inserted, which may have prompted the photograph, as part of the County of Avon's attempts to protect shopfronts.

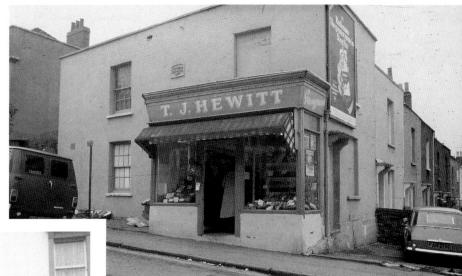

(256) October 1979: East Street Nos 114 & 116, EP Bryan, tobacconist and shell fish merchant, respectively in a pair of houses *c*.1840, the sole remaining early C19 pair in this important shopping street. As soon as a scheme for redevelopment came before CAP listing was requested. It was turned down on the excuse that the rear wall had been rebuilt. Such disinterest in the local significance of a building is now not unusual, one suspects on account of listed building rationing. As a result, the pair were demolished and replaced with a sad, ignorant sham. This was an inappropriate approach to these historic buildings.

(257) *c*.1979: **East Street** Former premises of ES & A Robinson, later Anderson's and now Cameron Balloons. Good metal fenestration in red brick and matching terracotta, remarkably unaltered. Left, East Street Baptist Church, *c*.1880, pennant stone. The listed public conveniences here were demolished by the City Council against the advice of CAP in *c*.1981.

(260) below - Early January 1979: Host Street Early C19 pennant stone warehouse shows its typical cast-iron and timber contruction, in this reduction of length for a vehicle turning head. This was an early part of the eagerly awaited Christmas Street redevelopment-grant formula by Moxley, Jenner & Ptrs. Now everyone bemoans the demolition of landmark chimneys!

(258)c. **August 1979: Colston & Trenchard Streets** on a Sunday morning. The Griffin PH will grow an iron balcony on its prow, a seeming memory of Steep Street which curved up here [**11/34**]. Behind is Oatley & Lawrence's YMCA, then still emblazoned, not listed despite its dignity and facing an uncertain future. Distant in Trenchard St is the Catholic church soon to be faced as one element in the Lodge Street formula.

(259) 1965: Host Street Looking east at the warehouse seen in (**260**), then used by Bristol Tramways. Another pennant stone warehouse to right now demolished; note too the coal lorry.

(261) December 1979: Lodge Street Paty's *c*.1780 terrace awaiting refurbishment as flats with Joint Conservation Programme grant, following its salvation from office development at public inquiry years previously. Rebuilding of the west side on under-used land may follow closure of the street to vehicles.

A reader, Charles Mutch, wrote to RW in February 1977 with this recollection of Lodge Street. 'I was born at No.7 Lodge Street [in] 1904 [the double-fronted house to left of camera], but we left when I was still very young... Somewhere at the bottom end of Lodge Street was a Salvation Army place where poor children were given bread and dripping, and mugs of soup or cocoa. No. 7 was a theatrical boarding house, kept by Mrs Pierce and her daughters Mabel and Emily - a sailor son was drowned in the docks... No. 7 had a back garden of some sort and Mrs Pierce kept hens... One day I rushed out of the front door bang into the railings! It did not improve my looks... But the good ladies of the house washed me down and gave me my 'comforter', which was sugar and dried fruit tied up in a rag for me to suck...'

(262) Early January 1979: Colston Street A most welcome scheme by Peter Ware to refurbish this listed C17 row with Joint Conservation Programme grant will soon get under way.

(264) September 1979: King Street The Old Vic foyer in Halfpenny's Coopers' Hall of 1743/4. This conversion by a modernist architect was never a happy one, making a nonsense of the great Georgian guildhall. The exterior has been cleaned recently with Scheduled Monument consent. Will the Theatre's forthcoming Lottery application include putting the stair in the bay beyond the main space to properly reinstate this great room?

(263) 10 December 1979: St Jude's Bristol City Mission: non-conformity in 1950's Civic style. Morning and evening Sunday services are advertised.

(264A) 1979: The Downs National Westminster Bank took a speculative office building, left, which subverted a small and discreet Georgian enclave for offices before conservation area designation. Centre, former National School, with diaper roof. Right, La Trobe's debased terrace to Blackboy Hill of 1897 in yellow terracotta.

(265) 1979: Blackboy Hill Interior view of the C19 urinal adjacent the Memorial Fountain. The pierced cast-iron panels are clogged with paint and overrun with the usual (male) graffiti. A minimalist design; the roof and panel support tubes, it appears, may also be downpipes.

(266) 1979: Hartcliffe One of several shots on Avon County's file of what appears to be an early instance of public participation in the planning process. Paper cut-outs of houses are shown variously arranged amidst a residents' discussion group.

(267) 1979: Windmill Hill This slide of the plan of the Community Garden on the Windmill Hill City Farm site marks in white and grey garden plots, divided by narrow paths (same tone here) and compost, trees and water tap. The view looks south-west over Brussel sprouts and Whitehouse Lane to Victoria Park beyond. We would welcome photographs of the City Farm for the Archive.

(268) 1979: Queen Square The broken through diagonal ends of the Square deserve to be infilled, and not left open simply to see, from within, St Mary Redcliffe! Note here how the Georgian conception is destroyed. The 1959 Olivetti building, centre, is currently being rebuilt. We hope thoughts of underground car parking through this medieval refuse tip that helped fill the marsh have been dropped.

(269) 1979: Canon's Road The trimaran *Promenade*, designed by Nigel Irens, is craned from the Dome (**146**) into the Docks.

(270) 1979: St Augustine's Reach Port of Bristol taking depth soundings. Beyond is the then Exhibition Centre, in U & V Sheds. These are presently the subject of redevelopment proposals of a most undesirable kind. Conservationists are unanimous in insisting that this impressive group on the Reach is not reduced, but simply upgraded as at E Shed, in order to maintain this characteristic conservation area.

(271) May 1980: Tableau for Brandon Hill Nature Park at the *20 Ideas* exhibition.

Conservation Issues

Blaise Castle repairs

Brunswick Square: facading & double-fronted redevelopment of south side

Cumberland Street: demolition & redevelopment of north side

Church Lane: **St Michael's Rectory** & nearby **Manor House 58-66 Colston Street**

Broad Plain: demolition & redevelopment Goldsmith's House

Portland Square: Former hostel on south side

Richmond Terrace, blitz gaps

W Shed

Blackfriars: application to demolish C17 house

5-9 Broad Plain; listed No. 5 mostly demolished on account of owner's neglect, probably needlessly

31 King Street, grade II, C17 fabric thrown out in conversion to new restaurant; rescued from skip

Merchants Road: Pumphouse converted to PH

Civic Cross, Berkeley Square, consolidated by conservator-mason

Cathedral: sculpture set up incongruously before west front

Author joins Bristol (CAP) as SPAB representative

New building in progress

A4: Canopy under Suspension Bridge

Temple Street: London Life Assur.

Narrow Quay: Narrow Quay House

Charles Street: Sun Assurance extension

St John's Square, Bedminster & Rownham Mead housing

Feeder Road and York Road, industrial units

January

70-72 York Road collapse into Whitehouse Street

Concorde reopens as cinema

Lulsgate airport: Civic Society advises that expansion should be limited to charter market in order to stay profitable

Council proposes City Heritage Walk

Former Rectory, St Michael's: conversion to flats opposed by CAP

Government increase gas prices 30%

Secondary picketing case results in future legislation

February

Whitchurch airfield: hangars dem.

New roundabouts at Frenchay Park Road and St John's Lane

Lower Cheltenham Place: 2nd attempt to obtain demolition consent; partial demolition without consent in October

196-241 Hotwell Road demolished

Trinity Methodist church, Whiteladies Road: belfry re-erected on corner of Westfield Park

March

Gaumont cinema closes

Metropole cinema now a furniture store

Vandalproof pillar boxes added to some post offices

Robin Cousins wins ice skating championship and takes an open bus from Sea Mills to the Council House

Temple Meads Old Station:

British Railways agree to make Grade I (newly upgraded) building weathertight

Oakfield Road: Oakfield House, part gutting

Prince Street: Frank Wills' Seamen's Chapel demolition successfully opposed (but still empty 15 years later)

Narrow Quay: attempt to obtain demolition consent for No. 16, saved by the author and 2 others by the discovery that this may be the last surviving sail loft, its internal wooden columns and wooden crane partly burnt but

worth retaining. Receives Lottery grant 1995 for Architecture Centre

East Street: Weston's Art Nouveau shopfront at risk

Leek Lane: the Onion brothers, 4 french polishers, retire

April

20 Ideas for Bristol, 3rd exhibition, includes author's Prince's Wharf cranes for CDV and the first re-watering scheme for the City Centre; a scheme for Canon's Marsh; Corn Exchange Square; Glass recycling by FoE; Brandon Hill Nature Trail; and the Avon Metro, sponsored at 35 King Street Gallery by Comben Homes, busy building houses at Bathurst Basin

City Churches: Arts & Leisure Committee unsuccessfully urges Diocese to use available funds to keep all city churches for worship

Wilson Street: Nos 24-44 refurbishment proposed

St Paul's riots and street fighting, 2nd April, 19 police hurt

Bedminster Parade, Wixon's Kink demolished [**31/170, 38/33,34,95**]

Severn Barrage: Government interim report indicates it to be 'technically feasible'

Baltic Wharf: winning design for housing substituted by house builder's illiterate scheme, a forerunner of much else in the Docks

City Docks: Lifeboat Museum appeal launched & Nova charitable trust's *Pascual Flores* arrives for refit under a 16-strong MSC project

Avon Wildlife Trust launched by Somerset & Gloucestershire Conservation Trusts & Bristol Naturalists' Society with MSC help

Iranian embassy siege

May

Jacob Street: Former Rogers brewery, grade II, C19 & 20 additions

dem. & facades sorely used in re-use for Castle Gate & Company House development

Muller Road: houses demolished at entrance to the Rovers' ground

Avon Wildlife Trust launched, financed by MSC STEP scheme, aims to create and manage nature reserves, provide advice, educate, raise funds, promote enjoyment of wildlife and protect urban & rural habitats. Brandon Hill Nature Park is an early initiative

The Countryside in the 1980's, RTPI conference in Bath. Avon County proposes a 10-year landscape management plan for whole county

Stokes Croft Conservation Area proposed: CAP asks for Backfields warehouse to be included; declined. Later demolished without need being proven

39-42 Queen Square: Noddy style fake frontages proposed and built

Brunel House redevelopment scheme: CAP requests one less storey to Brandon Steep

Wapping Road: bland office development too high, but built

CAMRA group started to preserve character of PH interiors, oppose modernisation & unnecessary closure

Civic Society celebrates 75 years & publishes *The Fight for Bristol*

Mount St Helens volcano erupts

June

Newfoundland Road: extension to M32 completed

Hotwell Road/Merchants Road corner set back

Smythe Park, Dean Lane, grassed and tree'd

Kings Weston House: RW makes first overtures over future in respect of Police vacating; questions of security having to be repeated in February '95

Welsh Back: demolition of X shed

proposed for unsuitable design of squash courts

Avon Structure Plan, consultation draft

US computer sends out 2nd war alert in a week. Government annouces Cruise missile bases at Greenham Common & Molesworth

July

St Luke's Road: Wycliffe Congregational chapel demolished

Bristol Motor Co. leaves Ashton Gate [**26/176**]

St Brenda's Hospital to become flats

Ambrose Road, Crosby Row: CAP seeks reduction on 41 new flats & 8 EPU's

Queen's Road: Dingle's fibreglass pepperpot shopfront causes a stir, not for its covered walkway but for contravention of approved materials, eventually corrected.

Wine Festival has 700-ton Rialto bridge on raft as centrepiece

High Cross, Stourhead: SPAB opposes National Trust taking down for restoration. Damage ensues as predicted, NT unable to fund repairs and V&A seeks to take four statues for permanent exhibition and pay for replicas, in absence of funding from City

BR subsidiaries offered for sale to private investors

August

Rex cinema closes

'Friends of Blaise' established for buildings and planting

'Friends of Brunel's Temple Meads Station' established

Hope Chapel Schoolroom: partial demolition on safety grounds. In 1995 delisted as a result of the approved 1980 conversion

Bristol Rovers' stand burnt

Windsor Terrace residents adopt their road with setts, finished January '81

City Docks: E & W Sheds, Canon's Road, conversion scheme to arts centre and shops

City Docks: CAP opposes new quayside wall to Baltic Wharf

Redcliff Street: author identifies remains of C14 Canynge's Turris, Redcliff Backs, and in painting in Cotman exhibition at Art Gallery and re-discovers C14 Canynge's House arcade in Redcliff Street.

Robertson's Jam factory closes

Old Market: last pawnbroker, Raselle, closes (Reading said to be next nearest). Reopened later in Stapleton Road

'Sus' laws to be repealed

September

Environment Secretary withdraws £200m government money from local councils

October

St Barnabas' church, Knowle, converted to elderly persons' flats

Victoria Street: Proposed facadism of Nos 84-86 for office development. Still decaying in 1995. Many glass plate negatives within saved from loss

St Augustine's Place: redevelopment of former Tramways offices for more offices involves demolition of remains of medieval timber-framed houses and over-development

University Road: new classroom block for Grammar School

Portland Square: redevelopment & restoration of Nos 31-34

Bath Road: crude new gates to St Mary Redcliffe cemetery, 'doing our utmost to maintain in a worthy condition', results in delisting in 1995

November

Cathedral school extension opened

King Street: east end pedestrianised

Cumberland Street: CAP opposes

developer's further demolition attempt

Gaiety cinema, Knowle, instals rising organ. Closes 1995

Canynge Square Garden Society fights to keep the original gas lamps

December

Entertainment Centre cinema, Frogmore Street, reopens as a twin

Pile Marsh bottleneck widened

Royal Hotel closes

Gloucester & Pembroke Streets: Nos 18-26, & No. 1 where author corrects scheme for glazing pattern. No. 24 ruined by the insertion of a steel frame the following year

Lower Park Row, Ship Inn: consent given for development at rear and partly masks No. 10, which had been saved with grant!

White Horse PH, W-O-T: death knell to old wing to right of PH; scheme acclaimed by CAP, just shows how wrong Panel can be!

City Churches: the following to be declared redundant - St Jude, Poyntzpool, by Gabriel with good vicarage; St John, Whiteladies Road; St Katherine, Redland

Suspension Bridge relit after seven years

Victoria Street: former Bristol Temperance Hotel on corner with Temple Street (blitzed) dem.

John Lennon shot

(272) 1979: Prince's Wharf 2 of the 4 cranes Nos 28-31, then newly transferred by lease to City Docks Ventures Ltd in order to save these most important landmark features of the City Docks.

They had in fact already been sold to a scrap merchant in Newport and the 50 Bristolians who made up CDV paid £100 each to pay off the scrapdealer. So far their reuse has proved impractical - the cabs are very limited of space, even if the winding gear were to be removed.

These electric and slewing cranes Nos 29-31 were made by Stothert & Pitt in 1949 and later upgraded to lift 3 tons at a maximum luff of 65ft. Crane 32 was supplied in 1950 to lift 10 tons at 55 ft. luff.

(273) August 1980: Downend Park Road, Horfield The rear of early C17 Downend Park Farm, a lobby entry house with central service, a plan associated with a stair turret in the porch entry to give independent access to rooms. Also important for having its surviving barn alongside, unconverted. Having been saved from demolition by a previous City Council tenant [**5/146**], it was brought to its knees by an over-ambitious development brief by the City Planning Officer. Subsequently bought by a private owner.

(274) June 1980: Blackfriars, west of Lower Maudlin St. Unprepossessing, this house was scheduled for demolition by the Hospital Board. In fact it was the remaining part of a C17 house, which pre-war had a fine Jacobean staircase [**18/45**]. Following on from 10 Lower Park Row and as a result of the author's reminders it was retained and restored by the Special Trustees of the BRI.

(275) 1980: Hallen Road A house, quietly implanted behind a stables wall, designed by the author.

(276) Charlton Road, St George The importance of enclosing walls: here to a Quaker-industrialist's house

(277)1980: Newfoundland Street
Demolition of No. 16, to be followed by No. 18 and the Albion PH on the corner of Stratton St. Although Georgian and listed this meant nothing in the wake of the M32. Islanding it may have been impossible, but there was nothing listed in Stratton St, itself now cleared, and this row could have become a dedicated route into Portland Square Conservation Area [**31/126**].

(278) May 1980: Queen Square
from The Grove. Piling through the medieval rubbish tip of the Marsh for office redevelopment; the case referred to in Michael Dawson's article and Avon Conservation News. The C19 Gothic Seamens' Chapel fronting Prince Street, newly saved from demolition, still hangs on today, no doubt rotting. Will that be said to be un-Georgian too?

(279) 4 January 1980: Tailors' Court from Tower Lane. Excavations by the City Museum of Nos 1 & 2 prior to an office development; the first excavation of an uncellared site within the early Norman town. The foundation walls of a putative early-C12 first-floor hall of some pretensions were found.

(280) 4 January 1980: Tailors' Court Shell canopy of the former hall of the Merchant Tailors' Guild, 1740, with St John the Baptist's crest and emblems with 'jolly' camel supporters, to borrow Maltravers Herald Extraordinary's apt description (*Heraldry*, 1989). Repainted since **3/28**. Translation, please, of *Concordia Paruae Res Crescunt*.

(281) October 1980: Redcliff Street One of the sites of the City Museum's Redcliffe Project, Nos 86 & 87, looking west, the surviving Portwall Lane property of WCA offices (facaded and enlarged in redevelopment) top left. A pre-C13 slipway was found and the development of dyers' houses traced from the early C13. Site of building 5 seen, with dye vat bases by sign.

(282) October 1980: Redcliff Street Private developers were not the only culprits! Nos 91-93 were allowed to rot by the County of Avon. The author tragically failed to have the carved corbel heads of a fragmentary medieval arcade behind one house retained in development (How on earth had it survived? see *BAIW 1981-85*, forthcoming). All this demolished by a subsequent developer for replica facades.

(283) May 1980: Victoria Street, workshops of *c*.1875 at the rear of Nos 18 & 20 seen from Counterslip. The larger row, Nos 10-22, was brought into the 1987 Bath Street inquiry equation, then subject of a separate inquiry in 1989.

(284) 1980: Victoria Street The rears of Nos 18 & 20 after unpermitted demolition. This fault was not countered when put to the 1989 public inquiry, but for the Victorian Society and for conservation in Bristol the outcome was most unsatisfactory.

(285) left - May 1980: Victoria Street The infamous listed row of Nos 10-22 [**38/381**] with the last tenant at No.10, right, formerly Platnauer Bros.' jewellers' emporium. An open, galleried plan, now steadily rotting. Consents were granted at the 1989 inquiry and subsequently; nothing has been done, no repairs notices served.

(286) 4 January 1980: Silver Street An unlisted Georgian house and shopfront, demolished for a parade of shops without study [**4/108, 28/46**].

(287) 1980: Tower Hill Rogers' Brewery from Castle Park during partial demolition for Castle Gate office block and strangely named Church House. Built *c.*1865, probably by WB Gingell, and at the time listed [**8/13**].

(288) 1980: New Street, St Jude's The Volunteer Tavern with green glazed tile ground floor on a listable, but unlisted, early Georgian house. Note the original mullion and transom windows at 2nd floor. The building was a touchstone, if ever there was, for the design of new infill in this beleaguered area.

(289) left - May 1980: Jacob Street Brewery before conversion. Consent given for new windows to be introduced etc. and no longer of architectural interest as a result - which is of course the real test to be applied at the outset. Why was it not?

(290) March 1978: City Rd Baptist Church, 1859, by Medland & Maberley. Intact interior; spot listed '92 at Vic. Soc's request and office development thwarted.

(291) July 1980: Stokes Croft Although declared a conservation area in June 1980, Nos 40, 44-48 were demolished. The replacement was one of the most badly designed blocks.

(292) *c.*1980: Old Market
Central Hall
Designed in 1924 by a Lord Mayor/ architect of Hull, from Kitchen & Gelder.
The hall, middle of 3 connected blocks, was the location of many great pre- and post-war meetings. After efforts to secure the building and prevent its sale into the wrong hands, it was demolished and redeveloped.

(293) May 1980: High St, Stroud
Meanwhile better protection of historic buildings was achieved up in Stroud, by the High Street Action Group, who sat-in on the roofs of a listed row against attempts by a shoe manufacturer to demolish a good Classical row. A legal action against repairs notice procedure changed the law; requiring consideration under listed building law before dem. could be entertained. The late Dougal Hunter of Bath and the author gave evidence at the inquiry and the buildings were saved.

(294) August 1980: Barrow Road The skew bridge and viaduct, looking north to Kingsmarsh House flats, St Philip's, 1837-43, demolished 19 September '93. A 2-year debacle and a public inquiry had failed to prove the skew bridge was not a Brunel prototype on a GWR/Bristol & Glos.Railway spur, designed to test this frequently used design on the GWR. Was it remarkable or not then that the BDC demolished it without recording?

(295) October 1980: Welsh Back A row of 3 steel and 3 timber-framed sheds demolished for leisure buildings [**11/51, 18/33, 32/139**].

(296) October 1980: Feeder Road Early C19 warehouses of pennant rubble with brick dressings to openings, rising sheer from the New Cut. Demolished and replaced with brick industrial units.

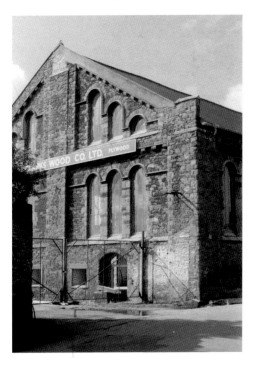

(297) & (298) October 1980: off Woodwell Rd Shirehampton This was the City Docks gunpowder magazine, a group of 3 unlisted Georgian buildings, then in use as outbuildings. The owner preferred dem. for spec. housing of this, the largest. The author's request for listing was refused and the smaller 2 were aggrandized out of recognition.

(299) October 1980: off Woodwell Rd The early C19 crane to the stone jetty. For a general view see *Images of Maritime Bristol.* p120, Elkan, 1995.

(300) & (301) October 1980: Feeder Road and Silverthorne Lane
Recent reuse of a listed 1870's manufactory by Clarkes Wood Co. The elevations facing the New Cut had unfortunately been lost.

(302) November 1979: King Street The Bicycle Exhibition at 35 King Street Gallery. An historical survey from Penny Farthings to design projects for plastic folding bikes.

(303) right - May 1980: King Street Transport Policy Machine in *20 Ideas for Bristol* exhibition. A spoof fruit machine on the apparent lottery of transport policies - aim: to halve the number of commuter cars parked all in Bristol.

(304) 1980: King Street Bronze doorpull for No. 35 King Street, designed by the author.

(305) May 1980: King Street 2 ideas in *20 Ideas for Bristol* - the author's rewatering of the Centre and reuse scheme for Cranes 29-32 on Prince's Wharf for CDV Ltd. [**272**].

(306) bottom - May 1980: King Street The sponsor's display in *20 Ideas for Bristol* for housing on Bathurst Wharf and Parade as envisaged by the consultant, described as 'Floating Harbour East'.

(307) opposite, right - August 1980: Bathurst Wharf The site of the proposed housing with the buildings required to be demolished. This might instead have been a massive reuse scheme of regional significance.

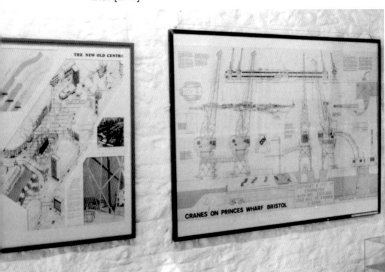

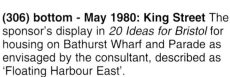

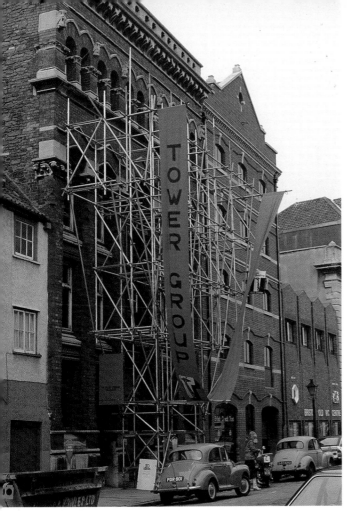

(309) October 1980: Prince's Wharf The sludge ship MV *Glen Avon* berthed alongside Z Shed (Y Shed behind), 1905-6 by Mouchel-Hennebique. Listing requests were rejected (another instance of inconsistency) and both sheds were demolished in anticipation of Harbourside. Foreground is *Räumboote* MV *Blitz* newly restored, long resident in the Docks (**74**).

(310) right - May 1980: Bathurst Parade Formerly Robinson's warehouse, 1874 by Lysaght & Gingell, was first facaded and restored with grant *c.*1981. In the late '80's it was refenestrated with a consent which was quite wrongly granted.

(308) May 1980: King Street Another idea in *20 Ideas* was a proposal that scaffolding of buildings should itself make a positive contribution. This scaffolding, by Tower Scaffolding for Keith Hallett, was such a demonstration.

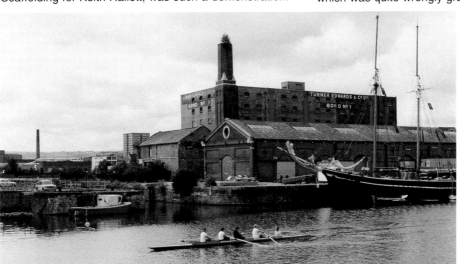

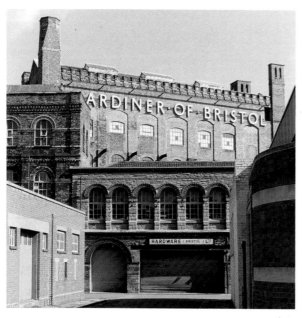

(311) October 1980: Old Bread Street Former Christopher Thomas soap works of 1881, by C Jones, after removal of the higher merlons, and before removal of the crenellated parapet [**38/75**]. For this most fabulous Bristol silhouette see [**32/142**]. Also former Thomas works in foreground, left, 1860 by Gingell; centre, 1865 by Foster & Wood; the subject of an unsympathetic scheme, *c.* 1992 at behest of BDC.

(312) May 1980: Queen Street from Counterslip Bridge. This was a particularly good and unregarded group rising directly from the Float and so redolent of Bristol. Hovis' mills and Avon Cold Storage, demolished for offices and flats, elegiacally called King's Orchard, in 1986.

(313) June 1980: Kingsdown Parade By 9 o'clock the Parade has been cleared (almost) of cars ready for the Street Fair.

Reece, his wife Dorothy and the author at the time...

12.50pm 21 October 1974 Reece at home sorting prints

10.10am 26 April 1975 Dorothy and her flower arrangement at the Bishop's House, Clifton

12.30pm 24 January 1977 The author with Citroen GS Estate

Index

August 1980: Day's Road, St Philips A fine classical cast-iron Bristol Gas Co. holder of *c.*1860 on a site not mentioned in Buchanan & Cossons' *Industrial archaeology*, and later demolished.

*c.*1980: Gas Ferry Road, development proposals wa ment and setted road sho Conservation Area – a me